Grassroots Literacy and the Written Record

STUDIES IN KNOWLEDGE PRODUCTION AND PARTICIPATION
Series Editors: **Mary Jane Curry**, *University of Rochester, USA* and **Theresa Lillis**, *The Open University, UK*

Questions about the relationships among language and other semiotic resources (such as image, film/video, sound) and knowledge production, participation and distribution are increasingly coming to the fore in the context of debates about globalization, multilingualism and new technologies. Much of the existing work published on knowledge production has focused on formal academic/scientific knowledge; this knowledge is beginning to be produced and communicated via a much wider range of genres, modes and media including, for example, blogs, wikis and Twitter feeds, which have created new ways of producing and communicating knowledge, as well as opening up new ways of participating. Fast-moving shifts in these domains prompt the need for this series which aims to explore facets of knowledge production including: what is counted as knowledge; how it is recognized and rewarded; and who has access to producing, distributing and using knowledge(s). One of the key aims of the series is to include work by scholars located outside the 'centre', and to include work written in innovative styles and formats.

All books in this series are externally peer-reviewed.

Full details of all the books in this series and of all our other publications can be found on http://www.multilingual-matters.com, or by writing to Multilingual Matters, St Nicholas House, 31–34 High Street, Bristol BS1 2AW, UK.

STUDIES IN KNOWLEDGE PRODUCTION AND PARTICIPATION: 2

Grassroots Literacy and the Written Record

A Textual History of Asbestos Activism in South Africa

John Trimbur

MULTILINGUAL MATTERS
Bristol • Blue Ridge Summit

DOI https://doi.org/10.21832/TRIMBU6805
Library of Congress Cataloging in Publication Data
A catalog record for this book is available from the Library of Congress.
Names: Trimbur, John, author.
Title: Grassroots Literacy and the Written Record: A Textual History of Asbestos Activism in South Africa/John Trimbur.
Description: Bristol, UK ; Blue Ridge Summit, PA : Multilingual Matters, 2020. | Series: Studies in Knowledge Production and Participation: 2 | Includes bibliographical references and index. | Summary: "This book examines how asbestos activists living in remote rural villages in South Africa activated metropolitan resources of representation at the grassroots level in a quest for justice and restitution for the catastrophic effects on their lives caused by the asbestos industry"— Provided by publisher.
Identifiers: LCCN 2019035911 (print) | LCCN 2019035912 (ebook) | ISBN 9781788926805 (hardback) | ISBN 9781788926812 (pdf) | ISBN 9781788926829 (epub) | ISBN 9781788926836 (kindle edition)
Subjects: LCSH: Sociolinguistics—South Africa—Kuruman. | Literacy—Political aspects—South Africa—Kuruman. | Evidence, Documentary—South Africa—Kuruman. | Asbestos industry—Health aspects—South Africa—Kuruman. | Asbestos—Law and legislation—South Africa—Kuruman. | Asbestos miners—Political activity—South Africa—Kuruman. Classification: LCC P40.45.S6 T75 2020 (print) | LCC P40.45.S6 (ebook) | DDC 306.440968—dc23 LC record available at https://lccn.loc.gov/2019035911
LC ebook record available at https://lccn.loc.gov/2019035912

British Library Cataloguing in Publication Data
A catalogue entry for this book is available from the British Library.

ISBN-13: 978-1-78892-680-5 (hbk)

Multilingual Matters
UK: St Nicholas House, 31–34 High Street, Bristol BS1 2AW, UK.
USA: NBN, Blue Ridge Summit, PA, USA.

The policy of Multilingual Matters/Channel View Publications is to use papers that are natural, renewable and recyclable products, made from wood grown in sustainable forests. In the manufacturing process of our books, and to further support our policy, preference is given to printers that have FSC and PEFC Chain of Custody certification. The FSC and/or PEFC logos will appear on those books where full certification has been granted to the printer concerned.

Typeset by Nova Techset Private Limited, Bengaluru and Chennai, India.
Printed and bound in the UK by the CPI Books Group Ltd.
Printed and bound in the US by NBN.

Contents

Acknowledgments

The first three people to thank for their help in putting this book together were key figures in the formation of the Asbestos Interest Group (AIG) in Kuruman, South Africa in late 2001 and early 2002. This book would not have been possible without the many conversations over the years with Richard Aitken, Sophia Kisting and Stephen Kotoloane. Each has provided key insights, details and clarifications, although they are not, of course, responsible for the interpretations in this book. I thank them all for their generosity, wit, kindness and hospitality.

There are many others to thank for interviews and conversations: Addison Oepeng, Brenda Sethibeng and Chalene Pretorious on the AIG; Tina Da Cruz, John Doidge, Jim teWaterNaude and Phiroshaw Camay on various aspects concerning the Asbestos Relief Trust; Judith Cornell, Mohammed Jeebhay and Elizabeth Nodu Nolokwe on the Industrial Health Research Group and the rise of occupational health activism in the 1980s; Barry Castleman on his 1983 visit to South Africa; Fano Endor on the workshops he led in 2001 for the Asbestos Collaborative; Robert R. Jones on his research with the AIG on secondary asbestos contamination; and Richard Spoor, who devised the legal strategy in the compensation case against the multinational corporation Gencor and its asbestos mining affiliates.

I am especially grateful to David Goldblatt for permission to use photographs from his asbestos series in this book.

Rochelle Kapp, Karen Press and David Johnson read all or part of the manuscript in its early stages and provided invaluable feedback and comradely encouragement. They are great readers and great friends.

I want to thank Emerson College for two Faculty Advancement Fund Grants which supported research trips to South Africa.

Jan Blommaert and Carolyn McKinney wrote the most collegial, intellectually engaging and helpful reviews of the manuscript imaginable. Likewise, the editors of the Studies in Knowledge Production and Participation series, Mary Jane Curry and Theresa Lillis, gave me wonderful feedback and encouragement. Multilingual Matters editor Anna Roderick has been great to work with.

Finally, I want to thank the three generations of my family for their patience and support. I am happy to say that this book is part of a larger involvement that began in 2001, when my partner Lundy Braun was a coleader of the US–South African student-faculty research project, and continues into the present in my daughter Lucia Trimbur's work on the historic silicosis compensation case that has just been settled out of court. Catherine and Rahul have been great supporters. Clare and Bob have been watching from the west coast. The grandkids are the future.

Abbreviations

AC	Asbestos Collaborative
AIG	Asbestos Interest Group
AKC	Asbestos Kgatelopele Community
ANC	African National Congress
ARD	Asbestos-related disease
ART	Asbestos Relief Trust
AZAPO	Azanian People's Organization
BAMCWU	Black Allied Mining and Construction Workers Union
BC	Black consciousness
BMRD	Batlaharo Mmogo Reka Dira
CAWU	Construction and Allied Workers Union
CCS	Conservation Support Services
CCOD	Compensation Commissioner of Occupational Disease
COIDA	Compensation for Occupational Injuries and Diseases Act
COSATU	Congress of South African Trade Unions
CPAA	Concerned People Against Asbestos
EKSCPA	Ekuiphileni Kwesive Songimvelo Community Property Association
GEAR	Growth, Employment and Redistribution
IHRG	Industrial Health Research Group
KMMT	Kuruman Moffat Mission Trust
KRT	Kgalagadi Relief Trust
MAA	Moffat Asbestos Alliance
MACH	Moffat Asbestos Claims Handlers
MBOD	Medical Bureau for Occupational Disease
MOSA	Machinery and Occupational Safety Act
NGO	Non-governmental organization
NNS	Ntuli, Noble & Spoor
NRC	Native Recruiting Corporation
NUM	National Union of Mineworkers
ODMWA	Occupational Diseases in Mines and Works Act
PRA	Participatory Rural Appraisal
PRU	Pneumoconiosis Research Unit
SAAPAC	South African Asbestos Producers Advisory Committee
SADF	South African Defense Force

SALB	*South African Labour Bulletin*
SALDRU	Southern African Labour and Development Research Unit
SAMWU	South African Municipal Workers Union
TLV	Threshold limit value
UCC	United Church of Christ
UCT	University of Cape Town

Preface

In the global north, late 20th century campaigns to ban asbestos recreated the personality of the mineral, changing it from the 'miracle fiber' of the post-war asbestos boom into 'killer dust,' a deadly pathogen that causes asbestosis (a scarring or fibrosis of the lungs), mesothelioma (a rare cancer of the lung's lining or the peritoneal cavity) and lung cancer. Starting in the 1970s and early 1980s, a powerful ban-asbestos movement formed in the Euro-American metropolis, consisting of activist scientists, physicians, public health workers, trade unionists, engaged journalists, public interest groups and concerned citizens. Megawatt legal cases bankrupted asbestos giants Johns-Manville in the United States and Turner & Newall in Great Britain, dooming the industry as a viable business venture in the north.

By the early 21st century, the European Union and over 50 countries had banned asbestos. In 2012, national and international pressure finally persuaded Canada, the world's leading exporter of asbestos for most of the 20th century, to stop the revival of asbestos mining in Quebec and disband its powerful asbestos lobby, the Chrysotile Institute.[1] In 2017, Brazil, the world's third-largest producer at the time, banned asbestos.

One unanticipated result of banning asbestos was that the felt sense of the mineral's presence began to diminish. As a banned pathogen whose market value had fallen to less than zero, asbestos seemed to recede from the public consciousness, eliminated as an active threat by enlightened public policy and decontamination campaigns that removed or contained the toxic fibers in the built environment. In effect, an abatement of attention to asbestos came about by the actual abatement of risk in the global north. The prohibition of asbestos recalibrated the temporal standing of the mineral, detaching it from the present and banishing it to the past. When the industry closed in the north, asbestos was reclassified as a tragic error, like thalidomide or DDT, and former asbestos mining communities like Libby, Montana or Wittenoom, Australia were turned, in the popular imagination, into ghost towns, faint reminders of the terrible blunders of the past, now rectified, which can safely fade from active attention.

The problem, however, is that once relegated to historical memory, asbestos becomes all the more difficult to see in its myriad manifestations in the present. The combined effect of banning-from-use and banishing-to-the-past has pushed to the margins of public awareness the active multi-sited persistence of asbestos and its deadly consequences: in Russia, Kazakhstan, China, and other countries where asbestos mines are still operating legally; in small, largely unregulated factories in Latin America, India, the Middle East and South East Asia, where asbestos manufacturing continues; and in abandoned places like the Kuruman district in South Africa – the site of this book – where the last asbestos mines shut down in the 1990s and the retrenched mining communities left behind face continuing exposure to asbestos and an epidemic of the asbestos-related diseases.

The point is that although asbestos has been refigured in the north as a dreadful mistake of the past, the mineral itself has not vanished. In fact, asbestos *cannot* vanish, since the mineral is an indestructible geological substance that does not break down or decay. To put it another way, as an imperishable mineral asbestos has an enduring semiotic persistence. Long after mining has stopped, its lethal meanings continue to unfold in variable, uneven measures of time – geological, historical, cellular. The silent, slowly developing risks of asbestos are based on intertwined periodicities: the geological permanence of asbestos fibers, the historical distribution of exposure through work and residence, and the bio-mechanisms at the molecular level of the asbestos-related diseases. Compared, say, to headline-grabbing diseases such as HIV/AIDS, Ebola or the Zika virus, the delayed tempo of asbestosis and mesothelioma is easy to overlook, since the incubation time between exposure and the onset of disease can be as long as 40 years or more.

So the problem of attention to asbestos, as Rob Nixon suggests more generally about the prolonged duration of environmental change, is one of *attention span* and how the velocity of a turbo-charged media of spectacular events overwhelms other temporalities. According to Nixon (2014), what remains at the margins of public awareness is the 'slow violence' of environmental disasters such as climate change, industrial pollution, oil spills, radiation leaks, species extinction and deforestation. Likewise, the 'slow violence' of asbestos-related disease, with its extended incubation time, makes it difficult to bear in mind, as public attention is pulled to more dramatic and higher profile diseases that appear to be more immediately urgent.

One of the central motives of this book is to make sure that asbestos is not assigned irrevocably to the past but to show instead how grassroots activists in the former asbestos mining districts of South Africa have grasped its active temporalities in the present, in the slowly unfolding violence of contamination, exposure and disease. The book examines how the Asbestos Interest Group (AIG) in Kuruman, a network of village-based affiliates, sought to make the risks of asbestos visible and to give voice to villagers' quest for justice – to hold the asbestos companies and the state accountable for the fatal contamination of the environment and the prolonged epidemic of asbestos-related disease.

We will see how, in the post-liberation period of the early 2000s in South Africa, less than a decade after the fall of apartheid and the first majority-rule government being elected in 1994, the AIG mobilized the paperwork of the metropolis for grassroots purposes. The new South Africa opened new prospects and new resources for representing villagers in the former asbestos mining districts. Through the AIG's participation in village-based and state-funded research on asbestos contamination, through the mass registration drives in which AIG community legal workers signed up villagers as claimants in court cases against the asbestos companies, and through many years of providing villagers with information about the paperwork of the compensation systems for asbestos-related disease, the AIG found itself, in the course of its activism, drawn into a range of documentary fields, textual spheres and rhetorical situations.

Overview of the Book

This book is intended to provide a textual history of the AIG's encounters with the modalities of mainstream literacy in rural villages on the margins of metropolitan modernity. The book traces the back-and-forth movement of written documents – work records, medical examinations, compensation claims, power of attorney mandate forms, consent forms, legal affidavits, academic research reports, monthly facilitators reports, household surveys, maps of secondary asbestos contamination and more – across social locations and spheres of influence in order to see how the AIG transferred metropolitan resources of representation to the grassroots level, for villagers to gain access to formerly inaccessible modes of writing and forums of deliberation and decision making.

The Introduction does three things: it explains the circumstances in which the book came to be written; it provides an overview of the AIG's history; and it outlines the conceptual frameworks and methods of analysis that I draw on to make sense of the AIG's grassroots literacy in its relationship with the official written record of mainstream modernity.

Chapter 1, 'On the Periphery: Life and Literacy in the Kuruman District', locates the town and villages in the Kuruman district geohistorically, as sites of peripheral modernity at the far edge of empire, world markets and global communication systems, where the AIG and the villages it represents are partially plugged into and partially bypassed by the knowledge economies and information flows of elite sectors in the metropolis.

Chapter 2, 'Asbestos Mining and the Written Record: A Brief History', examines how the asbestos industry managed its presence in the written record – in the bureaucratic paperwork of state regulatory agencies, in the advertising and public relations wing of the industry, and in the knowledge economies that determined the meaning and exchange value of asbestos.

Chapter 3, 'The Emergence of Asbestos Activism: From the "Period of Non-awareness" to the National Asbestos Summit of 1998', traces the emergence in the 1980s of a trade union-based occupational health movement and how participatory shop-floor research and demands for workers' control of health and safety provided a model for the AIG's village-based grassroots activism.

Chapter 4, 'Grassroots Activism and the Mobility of Documents: The Formation of the Asbestos Interest Group', looks at documents that shaped the AIG's early history, with a focus on how texts mediate the relationship between grassroots and elite sectors in the AIG's constitution, in its pamphlet 'Asbestos and Asbestos-related Disease: What Do People Need to Know?' and in its grassroots research of mapping sites of asbestos contamination.

Chapter 5, 'Insurgent Lawfare and the Gencor Case: From Asbestos-related Disease Sufferers to Plaintiffs', examines the AIG's immersion in the paperwork of a ground-breaking legal case against the multinational Gencor and the complex legal and rhetorical transformations of ex-mineworkers and surviving family members into clients and claimants.

Chapter 6, '"The Lawyer Stole the Money": The Political Economy of Certifiable Asbestos-related Disease', is set in the aftermath of the out-of-court settlement with Gencor, when the AIG's textual labor shifted from registering claimants to explaining the uses and limits of the Asbestos Relief Trust and the state compensation system. This chapter examines the tensions and challenges to its credibility that the AIG encountered, as popular dissatisfaction with the settlement, rumors and political intrigue spread in the villages.

The Conclusion, 'Grassroots Activism, Popular Participation and Contextual Spaces', steps back from the events in the AIG's history to consider how relations between grassroots activists on the periphery and elite metropolitan spheres of influence enable and constrain popular participation in addressing the catastrophic legacy of the asbestos industry.

*****

In November 2010 I attended a prayer meeting in Maruping, a village not far from the town of Kuruman, for Edward Mathlabane, who was a founder of the Ncweng community group and a member of the AIG executive committee. He had just died of mesothelioma at the age of 56. Stephen Kotoloane led the ceremony, the people sang hymns and family members and friends gave testimonials. Most of it was in Setswana but I could hear the word 'asbestos' occur repeatedly, in a beat of anger at the sacrifice of life and the sorrow of not being able to stop it. Towards the end of the prayer meeting, Mathlabane's sister closed her memorial by turning to me and saying to go back and tell people 'we are dying and suffering. The men don't live to 60, and they leave us widows and orphans.' What I heard, in the anguish of a too-early death, was the fear and anger asbestos contamination, Sophia Kisting and Elizabeth Nolokwe of the IHRG began a program, funded by the British Trades Union Council, to train health care professionals to recognize and treat asbestos-related diseases – to make health providers understand that asbestos-related diseases had been misdiagnosed for years and that they were living in the midst of an epidemic.[12]

The Asbestos Summit of 1998

The transition set in motion by the closing of the asbestos mines converged in the 1990s with the political transition to a new democracy in South Africa, creating new possibilities for asbestos activists and the occupational health movement. This is evident in the Asbestos Summit organized by the new government in 1998 as a national forum to assess the problem of asbestos in its multiple dimensions and develop recommendations as an agenda for action. The Summit consisted of representatives of the state, industry officials, union leaders, health professionals and community members. The proceedings of the summit reveal a sense of high anticipation that the new government would address what the *Declaration of the National Asbestos Summit* called the 'legacy of human suffering and environmental damage that we inherit from a century of mining and irresponsible use of asbestos, and the efforts of affected communities and workers to bring these to the attention of government' (National Asbestos Summit, 1998: 5).

One of the striking features of the Asbestos Summit was the fact that voices of villagers and workers were heard. Community representatives from workshops that met in each province in preparation for the Summit brought the perspectives from the shop floor and from villages and townships that Francis Wilson had found missing 20 years earlier at the 1978 'Economics of Health Care.' For example, Seyathie Mitha from the Northern Cape Environmental and Welfare Department introduced the members of the Northern Cape delegation by reminding listeners that they came from a 'forgotten province,' far away and hard to get to but the place 'where the real [asbestos] dumps are, and these are the people who live alongside these dumps' (National Asbestos Summit, 1998: 23).

Sophia Kisting was one of the organizers of the Summit, and IHRG influence – and more generally the influence of occupational health activism in the trade union movement – can be seen in the Summit's recommendations for community and union participation in public awareness campaigns, health monitoring, research on health risks, and rehabilitation. The IHRG figured prominently in several of the speaker's accounts of their experiences in the asbestos industry. Speaking on behalf of the new government's labor caucus, CAWU leader Fred Gona noted the non-awareness of the dangers of asbestos that prevailed in asbestos cement factories 'until the trade unions came into contact in the early eighties with the progressive NGOs. Particularly Industrial Health Research Group (IHRG) which is based in Cape Town, and other health groups in other provinces. It was through the IHRG's medical doctors, health and safety functionaries and researchers that we became aware of these dangers of asbestos' (National Asbestos Summit, 1998: 47).

Charles Kadalie, an electrician and South African Municipal Workers Union (SAMWU) member exposed to asbestos in Cape Town power stations, described his frustrating experience with faulty medical screenings and the endless paperwork of the state compensation system. There is a barely suppressed fury that the annual x-rays and lung function tests administered by city medical officers had failed to diagnose his asbestosis and the asbestos-related diseases of co-workers 'physically worse off than what I am' who 'are still working in that dangerous environment.' As Kadalie explains, it was only after his wife, an occupational nurse, arranged for him to see a hospital physician and eventually a thoracic surgeon that he was diagnosed with asbestosis in 1997.

Kadalie credits the IHRG's Jeebhay for demanding medical release of his x-rays from the city of Cape Town, which clearly revealed signs of asbestosis as early as 1992. He thanks Sophia Kisting for managing his health care and for telling him that 'if we wanted to take this matter further, then we would have to drive this process' and get SAMWU involved. As a result, Kadalie says, 'together we [SAMWU] embarked on an investigation, some research and awareness programmes of our own' (National Asbestos Summit, 1998: 36).

Kisting's presentation to the Asbestos Summit, 'The Heavy Burden of Disease and the Challenge to Prevent Further Disease,' linked the IHRG's two-decades long involvement in asbestos activism to the moment of political change and economic transition that marked the Summit, as the mines closed and workers faced retrenchment. She distilled the hopes of asbestos activists that with the new government the abatement of asbestos contamination, the treatment and compensation of current disease sufferers and the prevention of further disease were achievable goals. In recognition that the diseases caused by asbestos are environmental as well as occupational, she presented the growing sentiment that all asbestos-related disease sufferers should be compensated and provided with 'accessible clinics.' In keeping with the IHRG's emphasis on the value of popular knowledge, she called for workers and community members to be included: in 'ongoing participatory research'; in education, public awareness and health training programs; in an 'interdepartmental asbestos forum' to coordinate the various government agencies dealing with asbestos; and in the evaluation of substitute materials for asbestos in the manufacturing sector (National Asbestos Summit, 1998: 39–46).

Kisting was acutely aware of the retrenchment of mineworkers and the economic impact of mine closings in rural villages near Prieska, Kuruman, Penge and Msauli. She presented a central point of contention at the Asbestos Summit that not enough was being done in the former mining districts to include local villagers and retrenched mineworkers in the rehabilitation of mines and dumps and in the maintenance and rehabilitation of housing, schools and other buildings that used asbestos as a construction material. A number of speakers reinforced Kisting's concern that the skills transfer promised by the government had not materialized in the rehabilitation projects run by Eko-Rehab, the main government contractor located at the historically Afrikaner Potchestroom University. Longstanding resentments are evident, for example, in the remarks of Orbet Mehlo, from CPAA in Prieska, on Eko-Rehab's virtual monopoly on rehabilitation: 'The people request participation in the rehabilitation process for example on motivation for rehabilitation. We don't need the white Potchestroom University to rehabilitate these dumps alone. We are talking about Venda University, we are talking about Kwa-Zulu Natal University, why only Potchestroom?' (National Asbestos Summit, 1998: 23–24).

In retrospect, the point is not just that Eko-Rehab did not do enough (and perhaps could not imagine how) to include communities or foster skills transfer by training local people in the rehabilitation industry. There was a larger failure on the part of the new government to deal with the retrenchment in the former asbestos mining districts by developing long-term programs to involve community members, retrenched mineworkers and village-based grassroots organizations in the ongoing identification and rehabilitation of primary and secondary sources of asbestos contamination. Eko-Rehab continued the rehabilitation of mines and large dumps it had been engaged in for the previous 13 years. It was not until eight years later, in 2006, that Robert R. Jones' government-funded study of environmental contamination included AIG village-based activists as fieldworkers in the participatory rehabilitation research called for by Kisting and others at the Asbestos Summit.[13]

The Asbestos Summit occurred at a particular cusp in South African history, at a time of transition poised between the asbestos activism of the 1980s and the demobilization and cooptation of community groups, unions and civil society organizations that became the modus operandi of the ANC government in the 2000s, as it turned from the economic populism of the Freedom Charter to the neoliberalism of the Growth, Employment and Redistribution (GEAR) platform. As part of the ANC-dominated tripartite alliance with the Congress of South African Trade Unions (COSATU) and the South African Communist Party, the trade union movement lost its independent edge, settling into the post-liberation period as a stakeholder in the scramble for influence.

At the same time, however, as we will see in the next chapter, the Asbestos Summit, despite its legacy of inaction, spoke directly to villagers in the former asbestos mining districts around Kuruman, arousing local hopes and expectations that led to the formation of the AIG.

Notes

(1) Jock McCulloch (2002: 120–122) has contested Snyman's periodization, pointing out that F.W. Simson published an earlier paper on asbestosis in South Africa in 1928 and that George Slade, who had been a medical officer at a chrysotile mine in the Transvaal, completed his doctoral study of respiratory disease at the Amianthus mine between 1926 and 1930.

(2) Cape Archives, Cape Town, South Africa, 2/KMN 35 No. 3/13/2.

(3) As E.P. Thompson notes, the grassroots writing of commoners and working people, such as the widespread use of petitions, reveals the emergent presence of subaltern counterpublics on the periphery of the dominant print capitalism of early bourgeois society. Thompson never quite thematizes this kind of popular writing, but its persistence in his work, as evidence of the making of working-class consciousness, is telling. I owe this connection to Jan Blommaert.

(4) Cape Archives, Cape Town, South Africa, 1/PBG No. 3/13/3/1.

(5) Cape Archives, Cape Town, South Africa 1/KMN No. 4/2/5/1.

(6) The number of at least 20 new reports, editorials and letters comes from the list Barry Castleman sent me (email, 14 June 2014), combined with two additional articles I found at the National Library, Cape Town, South Africa.

(7) Barry Commoner, email to author, 14 June 2014.

(8) For background on BAMCWU and BC trade unionism, see Wits (2012); see also Ally and Ally (2008: 171–188) and Gibson (2008: 129–155).

(9) On the Penge strike, see Action Youth (1984: 5–6), Dempster (1984: 9), Makgabutiane (1984: 7) and Makgabutiane and Dempster (1984: 2).

(10) Judith Cornell, interview by author, 31 July 2013.

(11) Mohammed Jeebhay, interview by author, 2 August 2013.

(12) Elizabeth Nolokwe, interview by author, 31 July 2013.

(13) See the next chapter for details of this study.

4 Grassroots Activism and the Mobility of Documents: The Formation of the Asbestos Interest Group

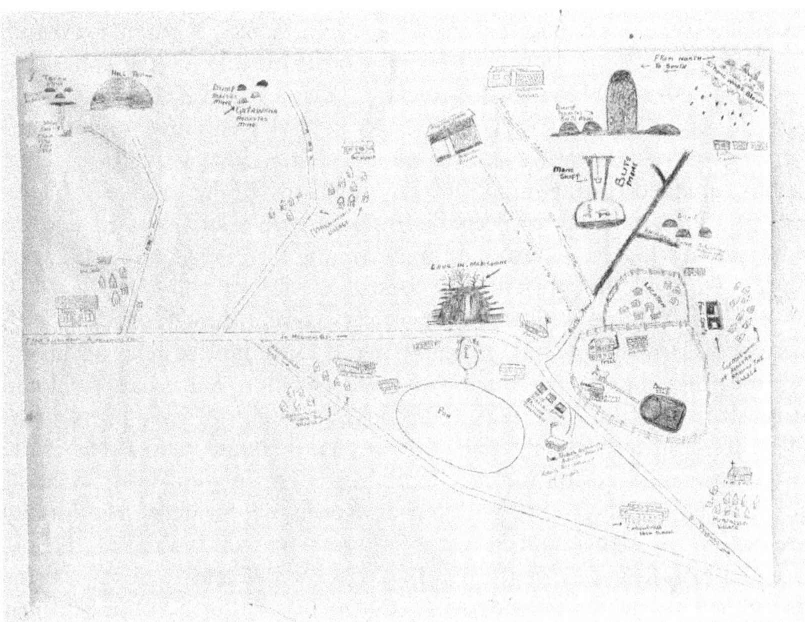

Figure 4.1 Photograph by David Goldblatt
A map, drawn by villagers, showing the occurrence of blue asbestos fibres around their homes and in their district, photographed at the Moffat Mission, Kuruman. 21 December 2002

The formation of the Asbestos Interest Group (AIG) was due in good measure to the efforts of Stephen Kotoloane, who lived in the village of Ga-Mopedi, a little over 20 miles from the town of Kuruman. Kotoloane never worked on the mines but was active in civic affairs and had been a lay minister in the Kuruman district since 1973. He was also a translator in 1998–1999 for the historian Nancy Jacobs during her research on the socio-environmental history of rural villagers around Kuruman.[1] According to Kotoloane, he became aware of the dangers of asbestos inadvertently when he showed Jacobs minerals he displayed in his home for their mysterious beauty, and they turned out to be asbestos. At the time, Kotoloane says, he thought of them as 'beautiful stones' and had no idea the blue fibers in the rock were dangerous. In any case, for Kotoloane, the 'beautiful stones' turned into what he called 'killing stones.'[2]

After talking with Jacobs about the dangers of asbestos, Kotoloane began to recall his experience as a lay minister meeting mineworkers at the end of their shifts, 'looking so dusty when they come out from work that somebody would have to show me the person.' He connected the exposures in the workplace he had witnessed to the health risks of asbestos-related diseases he just learned about from Jacobs. When her research in Kuruman ended in 1999, Jacobs left Kotoloane a book and some articles about asbestos. He says he was 'lazy' at times reading these unfamiliar types of texts but also was able to extract key meanings: 'sometimes I came across words that speak of people dying. How.' By 2001, when Jacobs returned to Kuruman with the Asbestos Collaborative (AC), an undergraduate research project she initiated with South African and US students and faculty, Kotoloane had already developed a local understanding of the lethal presence of asbestos.[3]

The birth of the AIG was part of a chain of events that began with Kotoloane's involvement as a translator and local intermediary at the village meetings the AC held during its research trip to Kuruman. As noted in the Introduction, the AC's visit converged with a wave of asbestos awareness and activism. By 2001, Edward Mathlabane, who attended the 1998 National Asbestos Summit, had already set up a local organization in the village of Ncweng, and Jannie Roodt was starting the largely Afrikaner group Kuruman Asbestos Sufferers in town. In Prieska, the historic Cape plc legal case on the part of Concerned People Against Asbestos was in full swing. The South African attorney Richard Spoor had just arrived in Kuruman, where he worked with AC members Scott Bulcao, a New York University law student, and Lucia Trimbur, a Yale sociology/African American studies graduate student (and my daughter), taking verbal testimony from asbestos disease sufferers and surviving family members and visiting village chiefs and other local officials to explain how a compensation case might be brought against Gencor and its asbestos mining affiliates Gefco, African Chrysotile and Msauli.

The two South African co-leaders of the AC – Sophia Kisting and Simphiwe Mbuli, who worked at the IHRG before taking a faculty position at Peninsula Technikon in Cape Town – connected the AC to the IHRG's occupational health activism of the 1980s and 1990s.[4] Most of the AC student researchers operated out of the IHRG office at the University of Cape Town (UCT). Kisting was the leading force in the project, orienting the American students, who were new to the politics of asbestos in South Africa, and defining the AC research agenda as an update on the implementation of 1998 National Asbestos Summit recommendations.

In the early stages of the project there was no definite plan concerning the written form the research would take or how it would be disseminated. This changed when AC members visited the parliamentary portfolio committee of the Department of Environmental Affairs and Tourism, and chairperson Gwen Mahlangu asked when the committee could expect their report. No-one had anticipated such a request or imagined that AC research would be given a hearing in parliament. The rhetorical situation suddenly became much clearer in terms of forum, audience and genre, but also more daunting.

In the next section, we will look at how the design and composition of the report grew out of the AC's tacit textual repertoire. Here we focus on the moment of delivery, when the AC's South African members presented the report to the parliamentary portfolio committee on 12 October 2001.

Delivery involves more than the transmission of a document. As one of the five canons of classical rhetoric, delivery (or *pronuntiato*) refers to the multimodal resources activated by the rhetor, including the pitch, force and velocity of the speaker's voice, as well as gestures, movement, eye contact, dress style, grooming, and so on.[5] In classical rhetoric, delivery emphasized the physicality of the speaker's body in the performance of the oration. More recently, postmodern and digital rhetorics have retained this emphasis on the materiality of delivery but have transferred it to the circulation and uptake of print and electronic texts, underlining the mobility of texts within (unequally) distributed systems of encoding and decoding.

The delivery of the AC report to parliament was enacted by a collective agent rather than a single speaker. The South African members of the AC – Kisting, Mbuli and the two Peninsula Technikon students Mpho Matsipa and Kagisho Motsemem – were joined by Stephen Kotoloane and SAMWU activist and asbestosis sufferer Charles Kadalie (who just appeared in the previous chapter). This particular combination of elite and grassroots sectors was itself a performance, signifying that the report was based on an informal alliance across national borders and institutional locations, between university-based activists in South Africa and the United States (represented by the AC members) and village-based and urban grassroots activists (represented by Kotoloane and Kadalie).

To put it another way, the delivery of the AC report to parliament carried Kotoloane along with it, transported by the trajectory of the report from the village of Ga-Mopedi to metropolitan forums of deliberation. If little ultimately came from the government's side as a result of the report, the moment of delivery nonetheless heightened Kotoloane's sense of urgency: 'when we came back from parliament we decided we can't just sit back and wait for the results. Something must be done.' Right away, Kotoloane telephoned Kisting. As Kotoloane notes, their conversation was pivotal in forming the AIG:

> So I called Dr. Sophie Kisting and asked her is there no way we can start a campaign of awareness to communities. She said yes but it would be very expensive because it would need money and there is no money. The best thing you could do, she advised me, is to write down what you think could be done and maybe we could try and find funds. And most probably kept contact with her all the time and in the meantime I started forming the committees in the very five villages. We formed committees at Sedibeng, at Ncweng, at Seven Miles, at Ga-Mopedi, Lokaleng. There was already a committee at Ncweng.[6]

The conversation between Kotoloane and Kisting linked the union-based asbestos activism of the IHRG to the village-based organizing in the post-liberation period of the 2000s. The IHRG's participatory ethos is evident when Kisting tells Kotoloane to make a list, to begin the process of inventorying and analyzing the current situation (the 'present troubles') and imagining what might be done. The AIG formed in late 2001 and early 2002. Within a year, the AIG had recruited over 80 villages.

This chapter traces how the AIG absorbed the experience of asbestos activism in the struggle years of the 1980s. Through its contacts with trade unionists, radical health professionals, community organizers, labor lawyers and activist academics, the AIG translated the prospects of the earlier union-based occupational health activism in South Africa to the new conditions of retrenchment. The AIG created a grassroots version of asbestos activism based in the rural villages of the Northern Cape and North West provinces rather than the workplace. Much as the shop floor was the 'fulcrum' of worker-generated knowledge in the IHRG's work with unions in the 1980s and 1990s, the village was the fulcrum of the AIG's community-based organizing and its grassroots research in the 2000s.

In this chapter, we follow the textual history of the AIG's formative moments, with a particular focus on three sets of documents:

- the AC report to parliament and the AIG pamphlet 'Asbestos and Asbestos-Related Disease: What People Need to Know' which distilled the AC report;
- the AIG constitution; and
- the AIG's grassroots research, as illustrated by the household survey which was presented at the Gencor launch and hand-drawn maps which recorded the location of secondary asbestos contamination.

The question that hovers over the chapter grows out of the dilemma of the AIG's grassroots activism, namely, how can an organization at the periphery, partially plugged into and partially bypassed by mainstream literacy, move the interests, experiences and aspirations of villagers across social locations, from the grassroots to elite spheres of influence?

The Asbestos Collaborative and the AIG: From Report to Pamphlet

The AC (2001) report, 'Asbestos-Related Disease in South Africa: Opportunities and Challenges Remaining Since the 1998 Parliamentary Asbestos Summit,' can be read, on one level, as a further realization of the vision of asbestos activism that Sophia Kisting outlined in her speech at the 1998 National Asbestos Summit, when she called for active state involvement, with union and community participation at all stages of policy development and implementation. Like Kisting's comments at the Summit, the AC report was attuned to the widespread effects of retrenchment and the subsequent need to link the devastations of disease and contamination to unemployment, poverty and social neglect. The legacy of asbestos mining, the AC report recognized, was not simply a medical or environmental problem but a larger historical disaster requiring progressive regional and local social reconstruction to deal with the closing of the asbestos industry in all of its ramifications. Above all, the report projected Kisting's optimism that, given the chance and resources, something could be done, that villagers and unions could work with the new post-liberation government to solve the problems left behind when asbestos mining ended.

In terms of the design and composition of the report, the AC's first visit to parliament activated the textual repertoires of the students and faculty involved in the project. This knowledge about writing operated largely at a tacit level, where semiotic resources had been naturalized as taken-for-granted forms of rhetorical agency and cultural capital. These means of representation were not so much waiting in the AC authors' rhetorical toolkit to be transferred to the new writing task but rather were reconstituted and *made available* to the AC authors as the pressure of the rhetorical situation triggered pedagogical memories of antecedent genres.[7] What resulted was the felt sense that the standard policy report, like those issued by universities, research institutes, foundations, think tanks, nonprofits and advocacy groups, with its central focus on 'findings and recommendations,' was the default genre setting. One of the report's authors described the process of composition as 'organic,' which indicates, I think, that the genre was never explicitly named because it did not have to be – because it was activated just below the threshold of consciousness as a variation on the familiar, deeply imprinted format (introduction, methods, results and discussion) of the experimental article and the laboratory report.

(1) To intensify rehabilitation efforts, with increased community involvement;
(2) To expand health services and medical surveillance, and remove barriers and inequities in the compensation system;
(3) To develop educational programs to raise awareness of asbestos and to inform local residents of their legal rights; and
(4) To ban asbestos mining, manufacturing, and import.

Figure 4.2 Main recommendations of the Asbestos Collaborative

For the AC, the rhetorical motives that gave rise to the report were two-fold: (1) to come to terms with the largely unrealized recommendations of the National Asbestos Summit; and (2) to serve as a conduit for the voices of villagers. In the first instance, the AC authors used the four commissions of the Summit as a template, or intertextual framing, to organize the report's four main sections and their findings and recommendations (see Figure 4.2). As a follow-up to the implementation of the Summit's recommendations, the AC report assumed a rhetorical stance that subordinated the assignment of blame for governmental inaction to the ostensibly more constructive motive of 'identifying barriers' and 'removing obstacles' to the realization of the Summit's recommendations. This rhetorical stance enabled the AC to affirm the work of the Summit by defining it as an unfinished agenda rather than a failure on the government's part.

On the other hand, the AC report also presented itself as a 'conduit' through which the 'voices in these rural villages' and the 'testimony of those living with ARDs [asbestos-related diseases]' could enter parliamentary deliberations (AC, 2001: 13). From this angle, the AC used the metropolitan resources of the academic research report to articulate the experience and perspectives of those who lived on the periphery. By channeling villagers' and workers' voices, the AC report recorded grassroots understandings that had long been overlooked or disqualified as irregular, naïve, non-compliant, ungrateful, or some other deviance from the mainstream epistemic register. Popular suspicions that the present state of affairs is rigged against those on the bottom have for the most part been filtered out of mainstream knowledge production.

To put it another way, the geohistorical predicament of the periphery possesses the rhetorical capacity to throw prevailing systems of meaning making into crisis by asking unseemly, indecorous, insolent or otherwise inappropriate questions. Sometimes, for example, a comment from the grassroots redefined familiar terms and opened alternative ways of understanding, as this quote from a worker in Cape Town does:

> The worst occupational hazard is not to have a job. (AC, 2001: 52)

A sense of frustration pervades many of the comments from members of the Ncweng Asbestos Committee, which formed shortly after the National

Asbestos Summit. One man noted the bureaucratic runaround the group had received from the government:

> It's years since we are talking about unrehabilitated dumps and still nothing is done. Each time we meet with someone, that one sends me to the next one, to Kimberley, to Pretoria, and still nothing is done. (AC, 2001: 3)

Another commented on the indifference and active discouragement of government officials:

> We have gone several times with this issue [secondary pollution] to the Department of Health but they are not so interested in talking about it. They have even gone so far as discouraging our committees from working with others because they say it lowers our dignity to do so. (AC, 2001: 37)

The mistrust of experts, based on the perceived social and epistemic distance between professionals and laypeople, is evident in this comment from Ncweng:

> When someone comes to look at our dumps, that person must not use a helicopter or a plane – he must rather come be a part of us. (AC, 2001: 41)

As the AC report notes, the racialization of the medical system and the loyalty of mine doctors to the asbestos companies have created suspicions among villagers 'about the loyalties of *all* physicians' and doubts that the medical services offered to whites and blacks are equal. The perception that whites receive better medical care and more diagnoses of asbestos-related disease, while blacks are sent to inferior doctors, misdiagnosed and given substandard treatment is the inevitable result of yet-to-be-dismantled racial divisions and hierarchies in South Africa. At the grassroots level, this mistrust of the system is not just a sign of alienation from the mainstream but also an analytical tool, as may be seen, for example, in this comment from a resident of Ga-Mopedi:

> We would appreciate it if all the people affected by asbestos, black and white, go to the same hospital. If there is one thing to be done, though, we need a clinic where both white and black attend. This would satisfy us that we are being treated equally. As it is now we see no whites at the clinic. Does this mean that whites are not affected? (AC, 2001: 54)

In the AC report, such observations serve, on the one hand, as data authorized by first-hand experience that reinforce the report's identification and analysis of 'structural barriers.' On the other hand, inflected by suspicion, doubts and mistrust, the words of villagers and workers inscribe a counter-epistemic register in the AC's report, a line of inquiry that begins with the question that comes, as we saw in the last chapter, from life on the periphery, namely '*how to get out of our present troubles*.'

When the AC report traveled to parliament, it was recognized as a familiar genre, its rhetorical status guaranteed by its realization of the conventions of the standard policy report from an academic research group. The mobility of the document – its capacity to 'have voice' across social locations – was never in question, as it moved from the world of academic research to the public forum in parliament, from one elite sector to another. The report, however, did not travel as seamlessly to the villages around Kuruman, where it loomed as a dense and difficult-to-read document, marking the semiotic distance between elite literacy sectors and villagers who were only partially inserted into the textual world of academic research reports and specialized knowledge. Reception of the AC report was variable: many villagers acknowledged its existence iconically, whether they read it or not, as a document that they knew spoke on their behalf. Others extracted salient points from readings that were necessarily selective due to villagers' partial familiarity with the genre. The mobility of the report, in other words, was real but restricted and largely unidirectional, 'globe-hopping' from one elite sector to another, university to parliament, carrying Kotoloane and Kadalie with it but partially bypassing the switched-off villages in the Kuruman district, precisely those places the AC report hoped to speak for and to.

Accordingly, shortly after the AIG was established, Kotoloane asked the AC to popularize the findings and recommendations of the report for readers around Kuruman, to turn a nearly 100-page research study into a short pamphlet the AIG could translate into Setswana and Afrikaans to distribute to villagers and township dwellers. I was the lead writer on the pamphlet in June 2002, working with Lundy Braun, Kisting, Aitken, Kotoloane and other AIG members, and with Lorato Trok and Chalene Pretorius from Moffat Mission, who were the translators. The 30-page pamphlet, 'Asbestos and Asbestos-Related Disease: What People Need to Know' (Figure 4.3), was designed and published later that year by Moffat Mission in three languages, with subsequent revised editions published in 2009 and 2014, mainly to provide updates on the compensation procedures that resulted from the legal settlements that established the Asbestos Relief Trust (ART) in 2003 and the Kgalagadi Relief Trust (KRT) in 2006.

From its inception, the design of the pamphlet entailed more than translating material from the report by condensing information and adjusting the readability index of the prose. It also involved mediating the discursive inequalities and epistemic distances that prestructured the production and circulation of knowledge about asbestos in the Kuruman district. A seemingly minor incident in the life of the pamphlet illustrates this point.

In discussions with AIG members it became clear that villagers were only beginning to recognize differences between the types of asbestos-related disease and that the biological mechanisms of these diseases were not widely understood. Villagers had been accustomed to thinking in terms of 'chest ailments,' which lumped together asbestos-related disease,

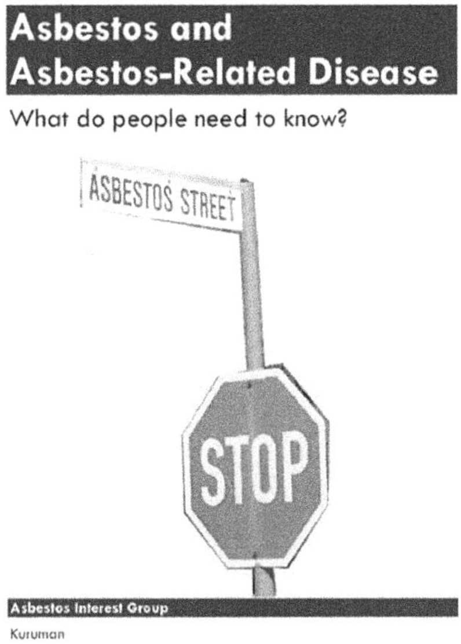

Figure 4.3 Cover, Asbestos Interest Group pamphlet, 2007

tuberculosis, asthma and other lung conditions in one category. This local understanding was the result, on the one hand, of the lived experience of villagers as they were forced to make sense of the host of respiratory illnesses prevalent in their communities and, on the other, of the systematic misdiagnosis, medical underreporting and restricted circulation of information about the asbestos-related diseases that created and maintained the distance between metropolitan bodies of knowledge and what people could know at the periphery.

The design of the pamphlet, in other words, was not so much a replication of knowledge that transferred information from one genre to another, from an elite to a popular register. Instead, it amounted more to a localization of knowledge that mediated elite and grassroots understandings, drawing on both to realign the unequal distribution of knowledge between center and periphery. This is why, for example, a diagram of the lungs (Figure 4.4) was added to visualize the location of the three asbestos-related diseases. A second diagram was added to illustrate the biomechanism of cancer as the proliferation of cell division. In both cases, the design motive was not to correct mistaken popular perceptions, as is true in many health education projects, but to unpack the possible meanings of the local term 'chest ailments,' in a collaborative undertaking to connect metropolitan knowledge and grassroots understanding (see, for example, Balshem, 1993).

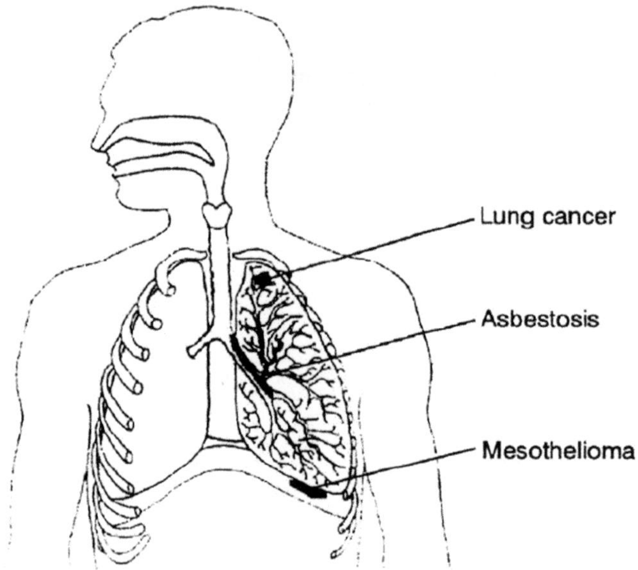

Diagram of the lungs and asbestos-related diseases

Figure 4.4 Diagram, AIG pamphlet

Making an Organization: The AIG Constitution and the Alliance with Moffat Mission

The AIG constitution was the outgrowth of a personal pact between Stephen Kotoloane and Richard Aitken, based on months of continuing conversations and common work after the AC visit to Kuruman. Kotoloane notes the moment when this relationship turned into the public alliance between the AIG and Moffat Mission and Aitken became the AIG's scribe, with his access to elite literacies:

> We formed a committee in January 2002, and we were looking for people who could help us get in contact with some government departments and so on. So we came to Moffat Mission and we asked the director whether we could hold our meetings here as a center. He accepted our request and we later asked him to be one of us, of our committee. And he so well accepted that and when we had to do some applications and write some letters he was the one to do that for us.[8]

Aitken, in Kotoloane's words, was the AIG's 'main contact person. Or a main messenger, or secretary, and adviser.' This was the division of labor that gave shape and energy in the early days to AIG activity, as Aitken used his access to metropolitan institutions and Kotoloane used his local knowledge as interwoven resources for grassroots interests. This was the matrix from which the AIG constitution emerged.

It is not unusual for organizations to exist, often for substantial periods of time, before their constitutions are written. The AIG, for example, had already organized nearly 40 villages by the time its constitution, which was dated March 2002, was actually published later that year. Still, what gives constitutions their special rhetorical force is that they signify the origin of the group, the moment of an organization's coming into being. Such 'constitutive rhetorics' of political manifestos, social movements and grassroots activism create not the organizations themselves, which can exist long beforehand, but the collective destiny an organization is meant to embody, emerging from the past in the name of a future already foretold in the founding moment. This is evident in the preamble of the AIG constitution:

> Whereas the lives of thousands of people in the Northern Cape and North West Provinces have been damaged through disease deriving directly and indirectly from asbestos mining over many decades;
>
> And whereas the lives of many people in generations to come will suffer disease deriving from asbestos mining and asbestos generally polluting the environment;
>
> And whereas asbestos pollution is a terrible scourge which characterises a vast area of the Northern Cape and North West Provinces;
>
> Now therefore this Constitution sets out the basis on which the establishment of the Asbestos Interest Group is effected.

The hand of Aitken, as the AIG's scribe, is evident here in executing the parallelism of the 'whereas' clauses, drawn from his memory of similar documents, as available means of representation to articulate the historic destiny of the AIG. The clauses detail in broad strokes the legacy of asbestos mining, propelling readers to the 'now' of the final line, the moment of origin warranted ('therefore') in the present by the 'terrible scourge' of the past, making the 'establishment of the Asbestos Interest Group' the lever to the future.

Constitutions are founding documents that codify an organization's mission, institutional structures and terms of participation. The AIG constitution follows conventional patterns of organizational practice. There are, however, three points in the constitution worth noticing for what they reveal about this formative moment of the AIG's grassroots activism.

(1) The terms of membership

The terms of membership specified in the constitution are based not on individuals who have chosen to join but on 'committees and groups from towns, villages and communities who have come together to express their concerns about asbestos and to do practical things about it.' The AIG was founded, in other words, as a network of groups representing villages and townships in the Kuruman area, not a voluntary association of individuals in Tocqueville's classic sense, who band together for a civic purpose outside the state and the market. No individual memberships were allowed. Nor did the AIG collect dues from the local village-based committees: 'No remuneration or fees attach to membership.'

This organizational design, as agreed upon by Kotoloane and Aitken, was important because it operated through existing geopolitical units instead of through an aggregate of individuals, thereby recognizing the authority of village chiefs, a number of whom became key AIG allies and helped to bestow popular legitimacy on the new organization. Further, basing the AIG on geopolitical units such as villages and townships rather than on individual membership emphasized how the asbestos industry had left behind a common danger affecting all who lived in the former mining districts, not an individual predicament or special interest. In this way, the village-based foundation of the AIG collectivized its destiny, positioning it to speak on behalf of the entire community.

Lastly, the decision not to charge dues for membership or fees for services was important in establishing the AIG's integrity in impoverished villages where economic desperation had produced a history of low-level corruption. As the AC report notes about grassroots organizations in the desperate time of retrenchment, '[s]elf-interested individuals may attempt to control organizations for the small financial benefit they might offer' (AC, 2001: 71–72). This was particularly true where government or grant money was involved. At the time the AIG was founded, charges of embezzlement and secret bank accounts had just been upheld in court against the local NGO Tswelelopele. In addition, everyone in the villages knew about unscrupulous claim handlers or 'sharks' who defrauded former mineworkers of their state compensation money or absconded with the money they were paid to fill out compensation forms. And there were vague rumors about sinister doings, such as the story circulating in Ncweng that 'money from Europe' intended for villagers was sitting in Kuruman, its distribution blocked by shadowy forces. Local scandals, small-time criminal hustling and rumor had made villagers deeply suspicious. Knowing these popular sentiments and the petty jealousies and rivalries they could give rise to, Aitken and Kotoane sought to inoculate the AIG against charges of corruption or self-seeking advantage by not charging dues or taking fees for services.

(2) Alliances with elite sectors

The AIG constitution expresses the will to form alliances with elite sectors, to link its network of villages at the periphery in South Africa to professionals in metropolitan settings. One of the AIG objectives, for example, was to 'seek academic partners to promote the collection and analysis of research findings,' in effect codifying as an organizational aim the alliance with the university-based AC that arose more or less spontaneously in 2001. Similarly, the AIG objective to 'appoint attorneys and advocates to seek compensation for damages for individuals through all legal means' gave codified expression to the AIG's involvement, already well underway, with Richard Spoor and the Gencor case. In both instances, Aitken used the prospective language conventional in constitutions in order to frame what were in fact specific projects already in operation, already connecting remote villages in the Kuruman district to metropolitan centers of influence and the cultural capital of its professional allies.

(3) The relationship of the AIG to Moffat Mission

The AIG's *relationship to Moffat Mission*, as institutionalized in the constitution, is the most complicated and problematic part of the constitution. It may appear at first glance an unequal one, with the AIG in the position of a dependent on the mission. The constitution stipulates, for example, that the 'AIG will not open bank accounts nor hold funds on behalf of its members' but rather appoints Moffat Mission as its fiscal agent to 'operate trust accounts,' to 'report to its members on the use of all funds' and to guarantee that all financial activity is audited. Furthermore, the constitution gave Moffat Mission the sole authority to appoint a coordinator to direct the AIG rather than making the position an elected one. In return, Moffat Mission agreed to 'provide accommodation and office space for the adequate functioning of the AIG.'

From one perspective, this may look like a paternalistic relationship that evokes the era of missionaries and natives. From another angle, however, we can see how the constitution used devices of colonial authority, still actively present in South Africa, to institutionalize an alliance between Moffat and the AIG based on bonds of mutual trust between Aitken and Kotoloane and their deeply felt shared conviction of the need for grassroots organizing and grassroots research to comprehend the dimensions of the asbestos catastrophe and to develop solutions.

The point to emphasize is that as long as Aitken was director at Moffat, the mission's apparently custodial relationship to the AIG, with its hints of the racial hierarchies of a discredited past, was meant to use the civic and religious auspices of the mission – what Aitken called Moffat's 'institutional virtue' – to warrant the AIG's incorruptibility and to buffer Kotoloane against charges of using the AIG for personal gain. The relationship was meant, that is, to counter at least partially the predictable jealousies and suspicions of corruption on the part of impoverished villagers when Kotoloane was paid a small salary as AIG coordinator. In what might look like a reversion to the days of indirect rule, when colonial officials appointed pliable native leaders, Moffat's power of appointment, by eschewing direct democratic election, was meant to depoliticize the position of AIG coordinator, helping protect Kotoloane and the fledging organization to some degree from the fractiousness of village politics. If anything, not having to run for office was an important consideration in maintaining Kotoloane's leadership and the AIG's alliance with Moffat, since Kotoloane was neither a former mineworker nor of local ancestry, having been born to a Sesotho-speaking family in Free State.

Ultimately, the terms set forth between the AIG and Moffat Mission backfired after Aitken left the directorship in 2003. As we will see in more detail in Chapter 6, the gamble of diverting colonial-era models to the opposite ends of empowering grassroots activism could not be sustained past Aitken. The new leadership that replaced him used the problematic terms of dependence in the constitution not as a privileged cover on behalf of the AIG but against it, to turn the AIG into a profit-making department of the mission rather than an independent village-based organization in an alliance with Moffat. But in the years when Aitken was director, the day-to-day alliance between Moffat and the AIG, with the participation of Kisting and more sporadically other AC members, was a secure and generative source of grassroots activism throughout the Kuruman district, based finally on no more than the deeply aligned affiliations and shared structures of feeling that arise from close, trusting common work.

Grassroots Research and Semiotic Mobility

The asbestos activism that emerged in the Kuruman district was from its inception an investigation at the grassroots level into the uncharted disaster caused by the asbestos industry. Before the AIG was founded, the Ncweng Asbestos Committee was already conducting grassroots research in a household survey of the presence of asbestos in construction materials. As we will see, the two main research projects initiated by the AIG were a door-to-door household health survey and mapping exercises that identified sources of asbestos contamination. Taken together, the two projects illustrate the uses and limits of grassroots research, both its realignment of knowledges and identities and its complicated relationship to knowledge production in elite sectors.

Marked by its grassroots origins, the capacity of research to move beyond the local level in globally remote places and gain footing in metropolitan centers was hardly straightforward for AIG activists. Rather, the AIG's grassroots research was caught up in the cognitive and textual hierarchies that organize the economies of knowledge and their exchange value in the dominant epistemic regimes of the metropolis. Transactions between periphery and center are constantly taking place, as Anna Tsing notes, but they are fraught with the 'friction' of inequality. The differences in mobility between the household health surveys and the maps reveal these frictions and how they enabled and constrained the circulation of texts across social locations and spheres of influence.

The household health surveys were simple door-to-door questionnaires that local AIG committees piloted in early 2002 (Figure 4.5). Kisting met

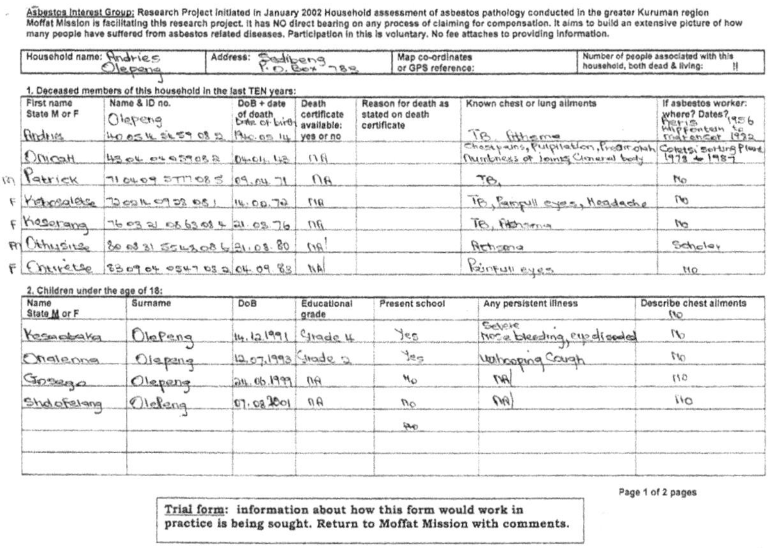

Asbestos Interest Group: Research Project initiated in January 2002 Household assessment of asbestos pathology conducted in the greater Kuruman region Moffat Mission is facilitating this research project. It has NO direct bearing on any process of claiming for compensation. It aims to build an extensive picture of how many people have suffered from asbestos related diseases. Participation in this is voluntary. No fee attaches to providing information.

Household name: Andries Olepeng	Address: Sedibeng P.O. Box 788	Map co-ordinates or GPS reference:	Number of people associated with this household, both dead & living: 11

1. Deceased members of this household in the last TEN years:

First name State M or F	Name & ID no.	DoB + date of death	Death certificate available: yes or no	Reason for death as stated on death certificate	Known chest or lung ailments	If asbestos worker: where? Dates?
Andries	Olepeng 40 05 14 5659 08 2	Date of birth 1940.05.14			TB. Asthma	Peris Hippfontein to Matenser 1956 1992
Omicah	43 04 04 0590 08 2	04.04.43	NA		Chest pains, Pulpitation, Prearoath, Numbness of joints, General body	Coletsi sorting Plant 1978 to 1987
M Patrick	71 04 09 5777 08 5	09.04.71	NA		TB,	No
F Kebosalotse	72 02 14 0952 08 1	14.02.72	NA		TB, Painfull eyes, Headache	No
F Keserang	76 03 21 0863 08 4	21.03.76	NA		TB, Asthma	No
M Othusitse	80 03 31 5543 08 6	21.03.80	NA		Asthma	Scholer
F Chuketse	83 09 04 0547 08 2	04.09.83	NA		Painfull eyes	No

2. Children under the age of 18:

Name State M or F	Surname	DoB	Educational grade	Present school	Any persistent illness	Describe chest ailments
Kesaobaka	Olepeng	14.12.1991	Grade 4	Yes	Severe Nose bleeding, eye disseded	No
Onalenna	Olepeng	12.07.1993	Grade 2	Yes	Whooping Cough	No
Gosego	Olepeng	24.06.1999	NA	No	NA	No
Shdofelang	Olepeng	07.08.2001	NA	No	NA	No
				No		

Page 1 of 2 pages

Trial form: information about how this form would work in practice is being sought. Return to Moffat Mission with comments.

Figure 4.5 Page from pilot version of the AIG household survey

with the AIG at Moffat on 25 March 2002 to review the trial survey, which was redesigned, adding arrows to highlight boxes for researchers to record additional information, making more prominent the place for the researcher's name and including a space for the date. The survey was then administered in May 2002 in Sedibeng, Seven Miles and Lokaleng.

We were staying at Moffat Mission in June 2002 when the survey results started to arrive. As noted in the Introduction, Lundy Braun took on the task of collating the surveys, making overheads and presenting the findings at the mass community meeting held at the Maphakela Centre on 22 June 2002, to launch the legal case against Gencor.

To be sure, the findings of the household survey were limited, based on 67 samples, far short of the 3000 Aitken had made a 'nominal target' in a 21 February 2002 letter to Kisting. It was not the number, however, but the results that mattered to the audience at Maphakela, enabling them to see represented graphically on Braun's overheads the ravages of asbestos they had been living with, the high incidence of 'chest ailments,' the vernacular term used in the survey.

As Kotoloane reflected on the survey and its presentation in a later conversation with Braun:

SK: So the committee started also, I think that is Lokaleng and Sedibeng, they combined it and they started a research on a door-to-door basis. And they brought that up and as they brought it up it was then to be professionalized. I think Lundy did that for us.

LB: OK, that's right. So that was the research.
SK: Yes, you prepared it to be in a much formula way. So we made use of that.[9]

The visual display of the survey results in Braun's tables and charts (the 'much formula way') mobilized the scientific authority of quantification to strengthen popular sentiment that restitution was due to individuals with asbestos-related diseases, whether they had worked on the mines or not. 'So we made use of that': the impact of the socially useful knowledge produced by Braun's presentation of the survey results may have been local, unauthorized on methodological grounds by its scant sample size and non-standard research design, but the results were telling nonetheless at the grassroots level because of the recognition on villagers' part of their circumstances of life.

To understand the fate of the AIG household health survey, we can say that its partial realization of the conventions of elite literacy, in particular those of the epidemiological study, limited its circulation, creating barriers across spheres of influence. The local category of 'chest ailments' that the survey used was unable to identify villagers' illnesses in terms of recognized disease taxonomies. Braun, as Kotoloane notes, could professionalize the information design of the data, but in the end she could not legitimize the research design of the study or endow the survey with semiotic mobility. At the same time, we need to recognize that these partially realized conventions transferred the prestige and epistemic authority of data quantification from center to periphery, giving value to local categories of understanding and making them available, via Braun's presentation, as popular forms of knowledge in building support for the AIG's insurgent lawfare.

The AIG Maps and their Circulation

The career of the AIG maps differed significantly from that of the household health surveys. Drawn by hand on newsprint, the maps displayed the grassroots origins of their coding system much more prominently than the household health surveys' local refraction of elite research practices. Despite or perhaps because of this, the maps proved to be more polysemous and more mobile, capable of being recoded to fit into varied epistemic situations and to move across social locations. In contrast to the household surveys, the maps circulated from grassroots to metropolitan purposes, from the periphery of the globally remote villages around Kuruman to the research design of mainstream science in Robert R. Jones' government-sponsored study, 'Assessment of Environmental Contamination from Asbestos,' and to the gallery exhibitions and art book publication of David Goldblatt's asbestos photographs.

The mapping exercises came from the five village meetings the AC held during its visit to the Kuruman district in 2001. These meetings were led by Fano Endor, who worked with Nancy Jacobs the year before on a student-based summer research project in Madagascar and who had been trained in participatory rural appraisal (PRA) techniques by Karen Freudenberger, an environmental activist with a long history of conducting PRA workshops for grassroots organizations in Madagascar and Senegal. PRA is a left-wing variant of rapid rural appraisal (RRA), a short-cut technique used by researchers and development workers to collect data quickly in remote rural locations (see Chambers, 1994). RRA developed grassroots research methods that involved local residents as informants but took the research back to the university, state agency or foundation to analyze. PRA, by contrast, was influenced by Paolo Freire's pedagogy of the oppressed and its vision of community research as 'conscientization.' PRA shifted the terms from extracting information from local informants to redistributing expertise, to turn rural villagers and township dwellers into grassroots researchers, to provide frameworks and tools to identify the sources of their oppression, to probe its causes and effects and to imagine possible action. This approach to community-generated knowledge was a good fit with the IHRG's participatory approach to occupational health activism and its emphasis on worker-generated knowledge, as represented by Kisting and Mbuli. Accordingly, the AC village meetings used PRA methods facilitated by Endor, primarily semi-structured interviews asking villages to identify and prioritize local problems and mapping exercises to locate sources of asbestos contamination.

The voices of villagers in the AC report to parliament come from these semi-structured interviews, but it was the maps that took hold in villagers' imaginations. Endor notes that some mapping of contamination was already underway when the AC held the village meetings. The mapping exercise at AC village meetings, he says, very quickly 'pushed past the simple level of an ice-breaker activity' accessible to everyone, moving rapidly from 'description to interpretation.' Villagers were 'very willing to talk, had a sense of what they wanted to tell the rest of the world, as though bottled up for a long time.'[10] The maps offered a space to explain to outsiders what the villagers were living with, to show the ubiquity of asbestos in the environment they inhabited, in the abandoned dumps, derelict mines and mills, roads, fields and buildings. The villagers took to maps as a representational resource enabling them to picture the sources of their troubles, to use the visual display of mapping to articulate their understanding of local conditions. Promoted by the AIG's local committees, mapping spread quickly throughout the villages, producing over 100 hand-drawn maps in the early 2000s.

The eye-witness observations of asbestos in the places where people live gave the maps their particular authority – and their hold on viewers' attention. As the geographer John Pickles notes in *A History of Space*, 'the map does not represent the terrain as such. Instead, all maps represent a particular image of the world that reveals the agency of the map-maker' (Pickles, 2004: 62). The rhetorical motive of the AIG mapmakers was to document the presence of asbestos and to show the world that people in the villages have to live with asbestos all around them. In this sense, the AIG maps represented in cartographic space the grounds of the villagers' grievances against the asbestos industry and the state.

Maps are multimodal compositions that combine verbal and visual codings. As Pickles says, 'the interplay' of words and pictures 'constitutes a distinctive image form in which the message is achieved largely in terms of the interplay and duality of graphic and linguistics meaning' (Pickles, 2004: 53). This intermingling of modalities – of caption and image – can be seen, for example, in the composition of the AIG map of Sedibeng (Figure 4.6), in which the meaning of the images is fixed by written captions such as 'asbestos school foundation,' 'asbestos in the yard,' 'asbestos bricks' and 'asbestos roofs from Merenco [Merencour] mine.' Even more, the reader's attention is circumscribed – and directed – by the arrangement of the captioned images and the density of documented contamination it produces, running in a horizontal band of contaminated structures across the lower part of the map to rise vertically along its right side past the 'graves' and 'asbestos toilet' to the dumps at Coretsi in the top right corner. The map image creates a cartographic sense of the ubiquity of asbestos, a feeling of being enclosed by contamination.

The five arrows at the top of the map, on the other hand, represent wind patterns and the direction of wind-borne asbestos. The arrows are what Gunther Kress and Theo Van Leeuwen call 'vectors,' or the visualization of action. The arrows enabled the mapmaker to interject 'narrative structure' into the spatialized distribution of asbestos contamination in the village, or what Kress and Van Leeuwen call 'analytical structures'

Figure 4.6 Map of asbestos contamination, Sedibeng AIG, c. 2002

that relate parts to the whole. The arrows interject temporality by showing how ambient asbestos is carried on the wind over time into the village (Kress & van Leeuwen, 1996). By giving the map image this temporal dimension of an unfolding event, the arrows signify the persistently active movement of asbestos exposure in Sedibeng, heightening the threat of asbestos-related disease coded in the analytical, spatially distributed representations of contaminated structures.

The AIG maps were of immediate use value at the grassroots level by identifying sources of contamination and thereby making visible the legacy of asbestos mining. In this respect, the maps played a key part in the AIG's coming to terms with a history that had been withheld from villagers. In discovering and representing this history, the AIG's grassroots researchers were operating, in effect, as what Phil Brown calls 'popular epidemiologists,' lay people seeking to make sense of the prevalence of disease by locating its sources, visualizing the impact of the asbestos industry on the local environment and formulating hypotheses that linked the localization of environmental pollutants to health effects (Brown, 1987).

The AIG gave the maps a historical destiny, to remap and hence to reoccupy semiotically the territory previously charted by the colonial powers that dispossessed the southern Tswana, separating town and village in the geo-racial configuration of social space known under the apartheid regime as the 'white spot' of Kuruman and the villages of the Bophuthatswana homeland. Part of the appeal of the maps to villagers is that it provided them, in the post-liberation period, with a coding system to reclaim their land, to rename its features and to rewrite its history in the cartographic space of the map.

Like the worker-generated knowledge of shop floor research, the AIG maps created original popular knowledge, an archive of grassroots research that documented sites of secondary pollution ignored by Eko-Rehab's government-funded rehabilitation projects, which focused on the primary sites at former mines, mills and large dumps. AIG mapmakers charted the neglected remnants of the asbestos industry in and around the retrenched villages of the Northern Cape, finding asbestos everywhere: in its use as a construction material in thousands of homes, schools, churches, government offices and other buildings; roads made of asbestos tailings; smaller unmapped derelict dumps; and the ubiquitous presence of ambient asbestos fibers in the villages, the playgrounds, nearby pastures where animals grazed and the open land of the surrounding vicinity. Hence, by mapping the secondary sources of contamination that only villagers knew about, AIG mapmakers amplified the potential uses and users of the maps. The maps moved beyond the local level in instances the AIG mapmakers could not have foreseen, entering the expert domain of scientific research and the artistic world of the distinguished South African photographer, David Goldblatt.

In the first instance, 11 AIG hand-drawn maps were integrated into the research design of the scientific study, 'Assessment of Environmental Contamination from Asbestos,' funded by the Department of the Environment and Tourism and conducted by Conservation Support Services (CCS, 2006), with Robert R. Jones as project manager. Like the occupational health activists at the IHRG, Rob Jones understood the value of participatory research, incorporating AIG members into the project as fieldworkers and collaborators. The local knowledge generated by the grassroots research of the AIG maps became a constitutive part of the research design: the project team compared the AIG maps to geographic information system (GIS) maps created from a database at the Department of Mines and Energy by Eko-Rehab. Based on a comparison of grassroots and expert knowledges, Jones and other CCS professionals worked with AIG participants to determine specific locations around Kuruman to investigate, identifying 80 sites of environmental contamination within a 5 km radius of 41 villages.

As the AIG maps were inserted into the study as sources of data, the modalities of grassroots research intermingled with EkoRehab's mainstream technologized science as a means to detect the presence of asbestos in the former mining districts. In this way, the research design functioned to close the semiotic distance between periphery and center, reducing the social inequality of local and metropolitan knowledges. As the maps moved across social locations, they took on new signifying power, entering into the epistemic setting of professionalized research design where the household surveys were unable to go. In the project's research design, the AIG maps were recognized as primary sources of knowledge, whereas the household surveys could never be seen as more than a partial realization of scientific research and its genres of representation.

In turn, the AIG maps were recoded, turned into quantifiable data in the determination of research sites. The maps were stripped of their primary visuality as hand drawn and observer based and incorporated into the professionalized scopic regime of the research study as units of information charted through GIS software against other technically acquired digital units of information. The maps, that is, circulated from the grassroots to the elite sector of government-funded research by undergoing a passage of form or remediation, a change in modality that enhanced their mobility and the value of the AIG mapmakers' labor at the metropolitan level of organized scientific inquiry.

By the same token, the AIG maps underwent a somewhat different transformation in David Goldblatt's asbestos photographs (Figures 4.1 and 4.7). As Goldblatt explained, 'After witnessing the excruciatingly painful death of a friend who contracted mesothelioma I did some exploring of the aftermath of the mining of blue asbestos in Australia and South Africa' (see Wits, n.d.). Goldblatt's explorations led to a sequence of photographs about blue asbestos which was exhibited

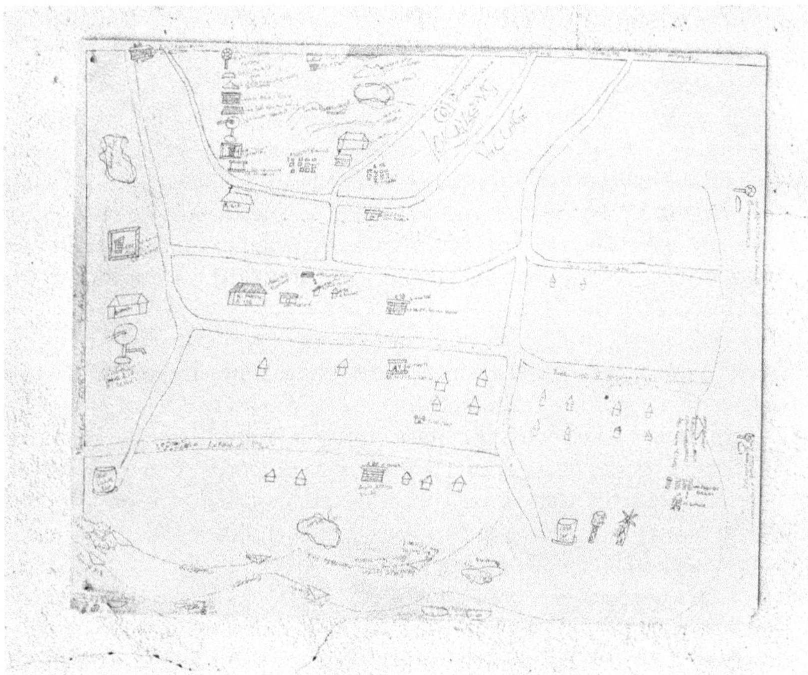

Figure 4.7 Photograph by David Goldblatt
A map, drawn by villagers, showing the occurrence of blue asbestos fibres around their homes and in their district, photographed at the Moffat Mission, Kuruman. 21 December 2002

initially at the Michael Stevenson Gallery in Cape Town in October 2003, in a grouping of 13 large color photographs including two of the AIG maps, and then appeared in a slightly different selection with one AIG map in Goldblatt's *Intersections*, a large-format art book which examined the conjuncture of political and physical geography in a range of post-apartheid landscapes and cityscapes, published in 2005 (see Goldblatt, 2003, 2005).

It is worth mentioning that although he had done commercial photography in color, the *Intersections* project was Goldblatt's first foray into color in his documentary photography. This enabled him to capture, for example, the blues of crocidolite asbestos and the neutral hues of sun-bleached landscapes in the Northern Cape. Color combined with the depth of field attained by Goldblatt's view camera to produce a remarkable level of detail in the asbestos photographs and an abiding sense of accuracy in his depictions of the legacy of blue asbestos mining. Goldblatt's commitment to accuracy is evident, furthermore, in two photographs of a tailings dump at Owendale, one taken in 2002, and the other in 2007 after the dump was rehabilitated (see Figures C.1 and C.2). The visual experience is that of witnessing what is available to sight, down to the finest details, as viewers see the blue asbestos fibers in the tailings field in one photograph and then the stalks of the grasses planted to reclaim the dump in the second. But the imperative of accuracy, Goldblatt explained, was political as well as visual, to document an instance when the government fulfilled its responsibility to people living with the dangers of asbestos by rehabilitating a contaminated field. To picture the abatement of exposure to asbestos, thereby, not only records the exemplary action on the part of the government but also serves iconically as a standard for future action.

In Goldblatt's photographs of the AIG maps, a semiotic transformation takes place much as it did in scientific study but to quite different ends, in a passage of material form through the technê or productive art of photography. Goldblatt worked with the master printer Tony Meintjes, scanning color negatives of the hand-drawn maps into a computer, with the screened images adjusted for darkness, contrast and color-saturation (but, as Goldblatt notes, only to the extent possible in the traditional darkroom and not computer enhanced). The photographs were printed digitally by ink jets onto cotton rag paper (see Haworth-Booth, 2005). As in the GIS software of the scientific study, the hand-drawn AIG maps were remediated – reproduced in a new form – no longer on news print but instead in art photographs to be hung on a gallery wall or printed on the high-quality pages of an art book, recoded as objects of aesthetic attention.

The visuality of the AIG maps, suppressed in the research study, figures in Goldblatt's photographs as a source of visual pleasure linked to the investigative motives of documentary photography. The photographs of hand-drawn maps seem to dwell on the mapmakers' means of inscription and their efforts, as Goldblatt mentioned, to render the three-dimensionality of the landscape in the two-dimensional space of the page, to locate the material presence of contamination as it occupies space in the former mining districts.[11]

Goldblatt's asbestos photographs were shot at the end-point of blue asbestos mining, in a time of retrenchment after the mines had been shut down and the industry left abandoned relics behind, both in the Northern Cape and at the Wittenoom mining village in Australia, the only major site of blue asbestos mining outside South Africa. Individual photographs explore the ruins: the derelict mill at Pomfret (Figure 2.1), the dilapidated former recreation center for white employees at Koegas (Figure 3.1), the Wittenoom asbestos mine in Australia, three men waiting under a tree on the heavily polluted road between the Bute mine and Heuningvlei, a deserted adit at the Langley mine near Prieska, and a man washing his clothes and children playing in a decommissioned mineshaft at Pomfret (Figure 2.5). The portraits of mesothelioma sufferers Ben Thorpe and Herman Kubari (Figure 5.1) and the asbestosis sufferer Boesman Kgololo reveal the ghostly pathogenic presence of asbestos.

The maps appear in the asbestos photo sequences as visual instruments of investigation, part of a grassroots inquiry that converged with Goldblatt's own explorations of the consequences of blue asbestos mining. If anything, Goldblatt seems to recognize in the maps a kindred motive to document, to bring to public attention the people and places where blue asbestos was once mined and still has a deadly active presence. In this sense, Goldblatt's photographs of the map images amount to an act of solidarity, of seeing *with* villagers the fatal distribution of risk the asbestos industry left when the mines and mills closed.

Notes

(1) The resulting study is Jacobs (2003).
(2) Quotes in this and the next paragraph are from Stephen Kotoloane, discussion with author, November 2010.
(3) Stephen Kotoloane, interview by Lundy Braun, 21 September 2003.
(4) The two American co-leaders were Nancy Jacobs and Lundy Braun from Brown University. Two of the students were from Peninsula Technikon; the rest were Americans, mostly Brown undergraduates.
(5) Delivery was the fifth canon of rhetoric. The others were (1) invention, (2) arrangement, (3) style and (4) memory.
(6) Kotoloane, interview by Braun.
(7) On the notion of antecedent genre, see Devitt (2004: 202–213).
(8) Stephen Kotoloane, interview by Lundy Braun, 21 September 2003.
(9) Stephen Kotoloane, interview by Lundy Braun, 21 September 2003.
(10) Fano Endor, interview by author, 2 July 2013.
(11) David Goldblatt, discussion with the author, 11 August 2013.

5 Insurgent Lawfare and the Gencor Case: From Asbestos-related Disease Sufferers to Plaintiffs

Figure 5.1 Photograph by David Goldblatt

Herman Kabari, who worked for a year in an asbestos mill, waiting for a bus to take him to work at an iron mine. He was suffering from lung cancer and mesothelioma caused by the inhalation of blue asbestos fibres, as well as from the effects of chemotherapy. He died at the age of 48 just over a month after this photograph was taken. Kuruman, Northern Cape

> We have had 3000–4000 claimants coming through the office – I am not sure anyone is keeping a daily tally. The vast amount of paper grows and grows.

These lines appear in an email Richard Aitken sent to Nancy Jacobs and Lundy Braun on 1 October 2002, to update them about the mass registration of claimants in the case against the multinational company Gencor and its former asbestos affiliates Gefco, African Chrysotile and Msauli. By the time Aitken sent the email, a small building that once housed the Mary Thompson Clinic at Moffat Mission had been converted into a Ntuli, Noble & Spoor (NNS) legal office and the AIG was sending out teams of community legal workers to local villages and beyond to explain the case and register claimants.

Aitken's email captures the mounting torrent of paperwork – the legal forms, client questionnaires, work and medical records and other assorted documents – that inundated the consciousness of AIG activists. This immersion in paperwork – the sensation of being awash in documents – was a defining reality in the formation of the AIG's identity as a village-based grassroots organization.

AIG community legal workers registered over 4000 claimants, extending legal representation to former mineworkers and surviving family members whose right to have their grievances heard in court had long been denied. The AIG's involvement in the Gencor case was the practical expression of an alliance with Richard Spoor, who masterminded the legal strategy, and its pact with Moffat Mission to represent the interests of villagers as the popular watchdog of the case. From its earliest moments, the historical destiny of the AIG was tied inextricably to the fate of the Gencor case and the out-of-court settlement that established the Asbestos Relief Trust (ART).

In the early post-liberation years, Gencor was a good target to arouse solidarity with those who worked on its asbestos mines and the townspeople and villagers who lived in the vicinity of its mines and mills. In the South African mineral sector, Gencor was known as the hardline Afrikaner outsider. Gencor was created in 1962 through a white economic empowerment scheme that Anglo-American's Ernest Oppenheimer brokered to create an Afrikaner-owned mining house. Gencor's appalling health and safety record included the 1986 Kinross fire that killed 177 gold miners, a flashpoint in the emergence of an occupational health and safety movement. In 1985, Gencor admitted it had installed a gassing system at its Klerksdorp mine to stun militant workers with nerve gas. As Laurie Flynn noted in 2006, 'When I think back to the many facets of the Gencor organisation that I have encountered in the last decade, it seems to me that Gencor is the most troubled, repressed and problematic mining organisation in the whole of South Africa' (quoted in Morris, 2006: 14).

The problem was that legal opinion in South Africa had long held that a 'veil of immunity' protected mining companies against civil cases for wrongful neglect. According to the prevailing legal reasoning, the no-fault provision in the state-run compensation system suspended the common law right of workers to sue employers, stripping them of *locus standi*, the legal footing to be heard in the civil court. In the annals of paperwork, the no-fault provision is a classic case of textual and epistemic blockage. In terms of knowledge production, it erects barriers to investigating the wrongdoing of employers in public forums by eliminating access to the affordances of civil law. The no-fault provision, in effect, restricts the circulation of worker-generated knowledge about health and safety in the workplace, keeping workers' lived experience and shop floor understandings from being examined under the law. In textual terms, the no-fault provision was meant to keep things quiet by blocking workers from testifying in court. The no-fault provision, in effect, presided over the absence of legal evidence about health and safety in the workplace. That, of course, was the point: beginning in Germany under Bismarck in the 1880s, modern industrial compensation systems were established in part to neutralize an emergent class consciousness of health and safety issues by trading statutory entitlements to scheduled benefits for a class peace that held no-one responsible for injury and disease in the workplace.

For Spoor, the Gencor case was a legal crusade to restore workers' common law rights – to lift the veil of immunity and secure the *locus standi* to bring charges against a villainous mining house. The motivating force in the case was the shared reckoning on the part of NNS, the AIG and Moffat Mission that the time had come to test the prospects of justice in the new South African polity – that a mass mobilization of neglected and desperately ill ex-mineworkers and surviving family members would make it impossible to ignore the scope of suffering and maintain the immunity of a now defunct and widely discredited asbestos industry.

The first half of this chapter examines the legal strategies of 'insurgent lawfare' in the two main cases against the asbestos industry during the early post-liberation era, the Cape plc case in Prieska and the Gencor case in Kuruman. The second half concerns the paperwork of the Gencor case and how the AIG's textual labor brought to the grassroots level the affordances of legal representation and the complex refashioning of villagers' identities as 'form-made persons,' clients and claimants in the bureaucratic mazeways of the law. As we will see, encounters across grassroots and elite sectors, as mediated by the paperwork of the Gencor case, were invested with insurgent potentialities but also prestructured by the asymmetrical distribution of rhetorical agency.

Insurgent Lawfare 1: The Cape Plc Case and the Question of Legal Forum

The notion of *insurgent lawfare* comes from John L. Comaroff and Jean Comaroff's analysis of the 'judicialization of politics' in late modernity, what they see as a 'gradual shift of the political – specifically the negotiation of collective rights, recognition, and interests, of sovereign self-determination, civic values, and the public good – into the domain of the legal' (Comaroff & Comaroff, 2009: 54; see also Comaroff, 2001; Comaroff & Comaroff, 2006). From one angle, lawfare is, in the Comaroffs' words, 'endemic to the technology of modern governance,' spreading the aura of legality to acts of state rule – of surveillance, coercion, dispossession and erasure. And yet, for very different motives, the Comaroffs continue, lawfare has also been used against the state as a 'Lilliputian strategy' – a 'deployment by "little peoples" against others more powerful' (Comaroff & Comaroff, 2009: 56) – mobilizing the forces of popular justice from below. This was the insurgent potential of lawfare recognized by grassroots activists as a means for ex-mineworkers to bring their quest for justice from towns and villages on the Cape Asbestos Belt to metropolitan legal forums.

There were two main cases of insurgent lawfare against asbestos companies in the early post-liberation period: the case against Cape plc, which started in 1997 in Prieska; and the Gencor case, which started in 2001 in Kuruman. The first was a landmark legal case against the former industry giant Cape Asbestos, a protracted six-year struggle in which the community-based Concerned People Against Asbestos (CPAA) and its attorneys Leigh, Day & Co. established legal standing to sue Cape plc (the corporate successor to the Cape Asbestos Company) in the British courts, in the country of its corporate headquarters.

CPAA formed five years before the AIG, in 1996, when ex-mineworkers with symptoms of asbestos-related disease began visiting the National Mineworkers Union (NUM) and ANC offices in Prieska, asking for help in applying for compensation and speeding up claims that seemed to be endlessly lingering at the Medical Bureau for Occupational Disease (MBOD) in Johannesburg.[1] CPAA's initial focus was facilitating compensation under the state system by arranging transportation for medical examinations at the MBOD, finally getting the system to pay ex-mineworkers' costs for the trip. CPAA also took up a campaign against asbestos contamination in the built environment which successfully pressured the new government to pay for replacement roofs.

In a research project at the Kimberley Hospital, CPAA worked with a Canadian physician, Dr Ahmon Randeree, who put the organization in touch with Richard Meeran of the London labor law firm Leigh, Day & Co. – the transnational connections that set the legal case in motion. The involvement of NUM and religious leaders as allies in the case and at least a tacit go-ahead from the ANC gave CPAA its political footing. Over the long duration of the case, CPAA remained animated by the justice of its cause, using, as Jock McCulloch notes, 'marches, vigils, and demonstrations as a means of generating publicity and maintaining community support' (McCulloch, 2005b: 71).

On the legal side, Leigh, Day & Co. had already devised the strategy of seeking to sue in the British courts multinational corporations that operated in southern Africa.[2] The legal novelty of the Cape plc case – and what distinguished it from the later Gencor case – was the question of legal *forum*, of holding Cape accountable in its corporate headquarters in London.[3] Leigh, Day & Co. argued that because Cape was a London-registered multinational firm and decisions about the mines and mills it owned in South Africa had been made in London, Cape should be subject to legal proceedings in British courts.

The question of legal *forum* – of where the case would be tried – was, in other words, not simply a matter of where the wrongful neglect and personal injury had occurred. The scene of the non-protection of asbestos mineworkers and their communities was clearly located in South Africa. The question of legal *forum* was rather a matter of the geohistorical relation between the periphery and the center – the fatal link put in place by the transnational supply chain that ran for over a century from the site of extraction in the far south to the boardrooms of the asbestos industry in the north. The legal strategy was to follow the paper trail from the periphery to the center, tracing the distribution of risk that had devastated townspeople and villagers in the former asbestos mining districts back to its metropolitan source, where the real power had been exercised and where accounts might finally be settled.

After a series of favorable judgments and reversals, the Cape case ultimately reached the House of Lords in a final appeal. At this point, the South African government intervened in the case, with the Department of Justice making a submission on behalf of the Cape plaintiffs to the Lords, arguing that the 'allegations against Cape did not take place in a legitimate legal system and the new South African government cannot afford to determine every wrong of the old regime through its judicial system' (quoted in Kazan, 2000). The South African government's submission brought the moral authority of the post-apartheid state to bear against Cape, holding that the 'discriminatory health and safety laws' of the old regime 'were against the law of humanity,' violating everything recognizable as the human right to a safe workplace and safe communities.

On 20 July 2000, the Law Lords ruled 5–0 in favor of the plaintiffs. The decision was hailed in South Africa and worldwide by occupational health activists, insurgent lawyers, engaged journalists, trade unionists and involved citizens as a victory for the ex-mineworkers and their communities, a legal ruling from the highest body in Britain that came to terms at last with Cape's habitual neglect and utter recalcitrance – that finally put Cape in its place before the court of law and public opinion in London.

This victory, however, was short-lived, as the case proceeded to an out-of-court settlement. Cape knew that it had no chance in a trial and agreed to a £21 million compensation settlement, to be held in the Hendrik

Afrika Trust, named after the first asbestosis sufferer in the case.[4] In any event, Cape defaulted on its first scheduled payment in June 2002, throwing the settlement into a crisis that was resolved only with the settlement of the Gencor case almost a year later on 13 March 2003. In the significantly reduced final settlement, Cape agreed to pay £7.5 million in compensation to the 7500 listed litigants, offering just over one-third of what had originally been agreed to.

Understandably, the case left bitter feelings in Prieska and nearby townships and villages.[5] Still, by upholding the right of workers from southern Africa to sue the mining companies, as Spoor notes, the Cape case 'has changed the way we look at occupational disease.' If the South African government supported the right of workers to bring the case against Cape to London, Spoor reasoned, it would be difficult to defend the longstanding legal immunity enjoyed by the asbestos companies in South African courts. After Cape, Spoor predicted, 'a wave of litigation against the industry should be anticipated' (Spoor, 2001a).

Insurgent Lawfare 2: The Gencor Case and Workers' Access to Common Law Rights

By the time Richard Spoor began the Gencor case in 2001, he had already gained significant experience in occupational disease law, working with Leigh, Day & Co. on the Cato Ridge mercury poisoning case and, for three years, on the Cape plc case. What distinguished the Gencor case from the earlier Cape case is that Spoor sought to sue Gencor in the South African civil court under the common law. The legal strategy Spoor devised was to go around the hopelessly inadequate and largely unreformed state workers' compensation system left over from the apartheid years to challenge the no-fault provisions that had long immunized mining companies. In a series of unpublished papers in the early 2000s, Spoor worked out the legal strategy for the case against Gencor.[6]

We will dwell over the next few pages on the intricacies of legal reasoning in the Gencor case. This is in part to recognize the ingenuity of Spoor's reading of the statutory law of the state compensation system and the close textual analysis and legal interpretation he advanced to lift the veil of immunity. But we must also underscore the fact that Spoor's exercise of legal expertise was enacted from a partisan position, as an advocate in the cause of insurgent lawfare waged with community allies to remake the prospects of justice for ex-mineworkers, their families and their communities in the new South Africa.

Spoor's line of legal reasoning was meant to intervene in the epistemic regime of the law by changing its ways of knowing whose voices can be heard in civil court. What made the lawfare in the Gencor case insurgent was its struggle to open formerly inaccessible legal channels in South Africa to the black rural working class, to those who had been classified under segregation and separate development as natives, subject to the customary law of indirect rule in the tribal authorities and thereby excluded from the rights of citizens under the common law. In the early post-liberation period, the immediate legal question of how to lift the 'veil of immunity' was caught up in the broader struggle to overturn apartheid's tribalization of black South Africans by extending universal human rights, full legal recognition and a non-racial definition of citizenship to all South Africans in the new democratic polity. The legal struggle for the common law right to sue employers for wrongful neglect took its insurgent force from this larger historical conjuncture.

Spoor began his legal theorizing with an analysis of the South African workers' compensation system. Confusingly, South Africa has two systems, one established by the Occupational Diseases in Mines and Works Act (ODMWA) of 1973 which covers only mineworkers, while the Compensation for Occupational Injuries and Diseases Act (COIDA) of 1993 covers the other occupational sectors. Under ODMWA, the compensation system was based on employer levies that paid a scant portion of the social costs of disease caused by the industry, providing ex-mineworkers with only a small percentage of lost earnings and limited medical care. As Spoor notes further, beginning with the Miners Phthisis Act of 1911, compensation was racialized, with drastically unequal benefits on the scale of 15:1 that provided pensions for white mineworkers but only lump sum payments equivalent to 18 months of earnings for black mineworkers. The greater part of the social costs of occupational disease was externalized to the ex-mineworker's family and community and to state welfare agencies, to be paid out of the general revenues without contribution from the mining companies.

Spoor notes that if the mining industry had been responsible for the full cost of occupational diseases, this would have exerted a powerful pressure to reduce risky exposures in the workplace (Spoor, 2001b). Instead, given the underfunded levies on the mining companies, it was cheaper to replace labor than to protect it, never mind improving workers' health or lengthening their span of productive employment. If anything, the longstanding doctrine of disposable black labor, compared to the costs of health and safety measures, operated as a disincentive to invest in the protection of workers' lives.

Spoor's analysis suggests that the underfunding of the compensation system depended not just on the paltry benefits it provided but also on its underutilization by eligible ex-mineworkers. Only a small percentage of black ex-mineworkers filed claims, received awards or had the free medical examinations they were entitled to under ODMWA's statutes (Roberts, 2009). Despite nearly a century of legislation, information about the compensation system was unequally distributed along racial-category lines, with most white ex-mineworkers having a general familiarity with the benefits to which they are entitled while black ex-mineworkers were bypassed. This lack of knowledge must be seen not simply as the inertia of an under-resourced compensation system but as a tacit policy in the political economy of compensation, a willful failure to inform sick and disabled black ex-mineworkers of their rights. After all, if the majority of eligible ex-mineworkers were to file claims, the system would implode financially. Instead, statutory entitlements went unrealized and the presence of many black ex-mineworkers went unrecorded in the paperwork at the MBOD.

The compensation system acted, in effect, as a subsidy to the mining industry, providing cheap insurance that enabled employers to dispose of their legal liabilities under ODMWA's no-fault provisions. Early rulings in the post-liberation period did not did not appear to be particularly promising in lifting the veil of immunity. A 1999 civil case for damages based on employer negligence, *Jooste v Score Supermarkets*, had been thrown out on appeal, the court ruling that Jooste had no standing to sue because Section 35 of COIDA precluded employees from taking their employers to civil court for occupational injuries or disease. The court ruled, moreover, that the loss of rights to sue for neglect was justified by the statutory benefits COIDA provided employees. Under the no-fault compensation system, the court emphasized, no-one – neither workers nor companies – could be blamed or held liable for workplace injury or disease.

As Spoor noted about the Jooste ruling, the trade-off of benefits for immunity was unequal and unjust, clearly favoring employers (Spoor, 2001a). By giving up common law rights in order to receive limited benefits, workers were thereby rendered unable to recover full damages for personal injury. Lack of access to civil courts in effect guaranteed that many disabled and sick workers would live out their years in poverty and neglect.

The crux of Spoor's legal reasoning about employer immunity rested on a re-reading of Section 100 of ODMWA which, like Section 35 in COIDA, had long been interpreted as limiting worker access to the common law. Section 100 of ODMWA reads:

> Notwithstanding anything in *any other law* contained, no person who has a claim to benefits under this act in respect to a compensatable disease as defined in this act, on the ground that such person is or was employed at a controlled mine or a controlled works, shall be entitled to benefits under the Workmens Compensation Act of 1941, or *any other law*. (quoted in Spoor, n.d., italics added)

Spoor argued that in Section 100 the term *any other law* was meant to bar workers eligible for ODMWA benefits from receiving benefits from *any other compensation scheme*, whether the older Workmen's Compensation Act of 1941 or the more recent COIDA. For Spoor, *any other law* referred to the statutory laws that established South Africa's fractured compensation system, not to the common law. According to Spoor, Section 10 could not preempt access to the common law because the statute that established ODMWA was of a different order or genre of the law, with no jurisdiction to curtail the operation of the common law. Spoor held that ODMWA was 'not intended to deprive persons ... of their common law rights' (Spoor, n.d.).

Such a revisionist reading, Spoor proposed, was potentially compelling on legal grounds because it was 'consistent with the canons of statutory interpretation that require that an enactment does not alter the existing law more than necessary' (Spoor, n.d.). If accepted in court, such an interpretation of Section 100 would remove the veil of immunity from the mining industry and establish the *locus standi* of ex-mineworkers to press charges against the wrongfulness of Gencor's asbestos operations. This line of legal reasoning, Spoor was well aware, remained unproven in South African law. And he realized that, for the case to succeed, it had to be a mass legal campaign, with thousands of claimants.[7] As we will see in the next section, the alliance between Spoor's law firm Ntuli, Noble & Spoor (NNS), Moffat Mission and the AIG became the vehicle of this mass mobilization.

The Gencor Case and the Alliance of Ntuli, Noble & Spoor, the AIG and Moffat Mission

The motive force behind the Gencor case came from an informal alliance between NNS, the AIG and Moffat Mission which materialized in an ad hoc convergence of circumstances that joined together its component parts in differently articulated linkages. For example, the link between NNS and Moffat was a cross-professional one, joining together the world of insurgent lawfare and the NGO sector of the new civil society in South Africa. Since NNS was, in effect, a renter at Moffat Mission leasing office space and incurring overhead costs, the terms of their relationship were in part contractual, mediated by memorandums of understanding about, say, who was to pay for repairs or utilities, as would be normal in the mainstream professional world.

At the same time, the relationship between NNS and Moffat was influenced by Spoor and Aitken's shared interest in radicalizing professional practice by aligning the expertise of elite sectors with the democratic possibilities emerging in the new South Africa. Invigorated by the prospects of justice in the early post-liberation era, Spoor and Aitken's activist bent made NNS and Moffat natural allies in the Gencor case, with a common orientation to link the powers and privileges of metropolitan credentials – from legal and civil society sectors – to the aspirations, interests and experiences of villagers on the periphery.

By contrast, the AIG's linkage to NNS was articulated across social locations in a number of guises – as community legal workers in the mass registration drive, as a plaintiff in the founding affidavit of the Gencor case and as the community signatory on the out-of-court settlement. In the founding affidavit, the AIG represented two classes of persons: those who have already 'been harmed by their exposure to asbestos attributable to the negligence of the respondents' and those 'who are likely to suffer harm as a result of their exposure to asbestos' in the future. The legal standing of the AIG as a plaintiff stood in for a category of persons not yet named but for whom the slow violence of continuing asbestos exposure guaranteed the onset of asbestos-related diseases into the foreseeable future.

The NNS and AIG linkage of grassroots and elite spheres of influence was evident, of course, in the mass registration drive, where the AIG supplied the textual labor that brought the paperwork of legal representation to the villages. But Spoor and the AIG also extended insurgent lawfare and grassroots activism to other theaters of operation. This may be seen in the July 2002 visit of Spoor, Kotoloane and AIG members Lorato Trok and Itumeleng Sithole to Heuningvlei, a former Gefco mill village about 130 miles north of Kuruman. The goal of the trip was to meet with the local chief and villagers, to explain the Gencor case and, if possible, to organize a local AIG branch in Heuningvlei.

The meetings at Heuningvlei led not only to support for the Gencor case and a local AIG chapter but also to a legal complaint, issued on 28 August 2002 by NNS, on behalf of the Bareki Tribal Authority and the Heuningvlei AIG, calling for Gefco to correct its 'perfunctory rehabilitation' of the mill site in town, which remained a source of asbestos contamination, and to seal the badly eroding tailing dumps around Heuningvlei. As Spoor, AIG activists and the tribal authority at Heuningvlei recognized, a protracted legal front in the campaign against asbestos needed to include rehabilitation of asbestos-contaminated sites in order to prevent further asbestos-related disease, as well as to compensate victims of asbestos after the fact.

The remaining link in the tripartite alliance between Moffat Mission and the AIG was based, as we saw in Chapter 4, on a pact between Richard Aitken and Stephen Kotoloane which was a deeply personal bond of trust to uphold the community's interests and exercise grassroots oversight of the legal proceedings in the Gencor case. As was true of Spoor's social partnership with the AIG, the linkage between the AIG and Moffat extended across spheres of influence. While Moffat Mission participated with the AIG in the common work of research and organizing at the grassroots level, its official standing as the Kuruman Moffat Mission Trust (KMMT) also provided access to elite sectors of civil society, especially in the religious domain, where the expectation, as exemplified by Bishop Desmond Tutu and others, that church leaders would speak out on morally compelling social issues was particularly compelling in the early post-liberation period. Moffat's history as a mission station and evangelical training school enabled Aitken, as KMMT director, to use Moffat's religious auspices – what Aitken called the mission's 'institutional virtue' – to vouch for the integrity of the Gencor case and the incorruptibility of the AIG.[8]

This use of KMMT's 'institutional virtue' evoked both Moffat's legacy of pastoral care to natives and its more recent civil society activism with its emphasis on restorative justice. In this sense, Aitken operated rhetorically both as the spokesperson for the moral conscience of KMMT and as the AIG's scribe, drawing on the resources of mainstream literacy to convey the AIG's interests to elite spheres of influence. Aitken's dual stance is evident in correspondence with church leaders at a particularly critical moment in the Gencor case. In September 2002, Gencor threatened to unbundle its interest in Impala Platinum (its only remaining holding in mining), distribute the assets to shareholders, and thereby evade its financial liabilities to claimants by de-registering and going out of business. On 1 October 2002, NNS filed a motion to interdict the unbundling. A week later, Aitken wrote to the Right Reverend Itumeleng Moseki, the Episcopal Bishop of Kimberley and Kuruman, asking him to act in court as the legal representative of a class action against the unbundling.[9]

The letter draws on Aitken's personal relationship to the bishop by opening in the direct speech of the first person familiar: 'I am conscious of the large and onerous task I am asking you to take on.' The moral proposition of the communication, delivered in the intimate register of a personal letter, comes from a collective conscience – a *we* that included the bishop in its assumptions about civic morality in post-liberation South Africa. 'The legal complexities' of the Gencor case, Aitken conceded to the bishop, 'are difficult to understand.' Nonetheless, Aitken writes, '*our* moral understanding is clear enough' (italics added). Here the letter moves beyond a personal appeal to the bishop as Aitken poses himself as the witness to a shared truth in the new South Africa: '*We* have, as *we* all know and quite rightly, entered an age of reparations for past evil' (italics added).

Aitken's appeal to the changing times in South African history evokes the rhetorical principle of *kairos* (from the Greek 'right time' or 'right season') which marks moments of heightened salience and moral urgency that cannot be ignored. Aitken mobilized the institutional virtue ascribed to Moffat in churchly circles to frame the issue of Gencor's unbundling as uniquely a matter of the post-liberation moment, of entering 'an age of reparations,' with its moral compulsion to address the 'past evils' of the apartheid regime. This rhetorical stance enabled Aitken to represent opposition to the unbundling as irresistible to the conscience of church leaders and all right-thinking persons, to ensure that the prospects of justice are realized in post-liberation South Africa.

The terms of the pact between the AIG and Moffat are given a particularly revealing expression in notes that Kotoloane and Aitken prepared for their joint presentation on the Gencor case to the Northern Cape

Provincial Forum on 25 September 2002 (apparently as handouts for those present) (Kotoloane & Aitken, 2002). Moffat Mission, for its part, the notes say, 'has undertaken to warranty the transparency and legitimacy of the legal process and, on behalf of our communities, attempt understanding of the immense complexities of this legal action in order that people are not deluded into false hopes and expectations.' The AIG, for its part – from an apparently different angle – 'is helping to give people confidence in the legal process.'

To prevent delusion but to build trust: the two undertakings articulated the problematic of the Gencor case for the AIG and Moffat. On the one hand, there was great concern about false hopes circulating in the villages, raising unrealistic expectations and exposing villagers to the unscrupulous promises of petty hustlers. On the other hand, for the case to succeed, there was a great imperative to establish its legitimacy in villagers' eyes. This shifting perspective of both working *for* the case, actively bringing the affordances of legal representation to villagers, and monitoring *the effects of* the case, to come to terms with its localized impact, can be seen in Brenda Sethibeng's description of her participation in the mass registration drive. 'We volunteered all the time,' she says. 'We went to villages. We spent days in villages for the registration.'[10] She notes that villagers were often initially wary of the AIG and 'not cooperative.' The 'reason is that they said this was not the first time that the registration process was in their villages. There had been people registering them, but for money. People took their money.'

The AIG had apparently been preceded by what villagers called 'sharks,' grassroots hustlers who had a long history in the villages of luring credulous ex-mineworkers to pay them to file claims and then disappearing with the money. As Sethibeng's account reveals, the Gencor case arrived at the grassroots level, not as a landmark legal campaign but rather as an occasion of petty criminality that tapped into the residual rumors and false hopes circulating in the villages that money for villagers' suffering was finally at hand. The task AIG activists faced was to establish rhetorical footing in the face of villagers' understandable suspicions: 'to explain to people,' as Sethibeng says, 'that we are not those people, that we are from NNS and we are doing this for the community.' The fact that the AIG, unlike the sharks, took no fees for registration enhanced the credibility of the community legal workers and helped to establish villagers' trust in the AIG's motives and build a popular confidence in the case.

The alliance of NNS, the AIG and Moffat Mission was a temporary social formation of differently articulated linkages across distinct spheres of influence. As a joint action, the alliance achieved its force not so much by functioning as a single unified entity but by operating translocally, across geohistorical tiers and their unevenly distributed means of rhetorical agency. If anything, these differences were crucial to the success of the case, as they endowed AIG community activists with footing in the villages,

Spoor with standing in metropolitan courts, and Aitken with influence in civil society – giving the alliance recognition and the right to be heard in multiple, normally disparate domains, from grassroots to elite sectors.

Paperwork and 'Form-made Persons'

The operation of paperwork in modern bureaucracies typically involves an asymmetric exchange in which record keepers fill in the blanks on a myriad of documents to create what Marie-Andrée Jacob (2007) calls 'form-made persons.' Under the refractive pressures of documentation, the textual labor of the record keeper bends and shapes the irreducible variability of an individual's social experience into repeatable categories, such as vital statistics, citizenship status, medical records, credit scores, certificates, degrees, licenses, benefit entitlements, tax returns, and so on. 'As acts of classification per se,' Jacob says, bureaucratic forms 'leave no place for overlaps between categories, instability, or multiplicity of meanings' (Jacob, 2007: 253). Rather, the person (and the very notion of personhood) in modern bureaucracies 'is not based on cognitive and humanistic understandings' but 'is constituted and preserved by legal and bureaucratic documentary proceedings' (Jacob, 2007: 250) – delimited and called into being by the blank spaces filled in and the boxes checked by record keepers.

Jacob's investigation of consent forms in medical settings reveals an important and perhaps unexpected connection between agency and submission in the bureaucratic production of 'form-made persons.' The terms may appear at first glance to be mutually canceling opposites but, as Jacob shows, submission to medical authority by signing a consent form also activates a kind of agency that enables patients to 'be moved along' through the system in pursuit of individual goals, such as donating a kidney or receiving a heart transplant. Submission, in other words, cannot be understood simply as an act of abnegation that nullifies individual agency but instead figures as a more complex 'expression of one's subjectivity' (Jacob, 2007: 260). Submission, that is, involves the transmission of a motive, as in the South African government's submission to the House of Lords in the Cape plc case, the submission of a petition by a citizens group or the submission of a manuscript in academic and literary publishing. If a 'form-made person's' subjectivity is the internalized recognition of bureaucratic categories, nonetheless, as Jacob suggests, 'submission and agency are not in a zero-sum relationship' (Jacob, 2007: 264). Rather, they are linked dialectically, with each term qualifying the uses and limits of the other.

These dynamics of agency and submission are evident in the paperwork of the mass registration drive in the Gencor case. AIG activists provided the textual labor, translating and explaining at the grassroots level a series of legal forms designed by NNS. This paperwork produced 'form-made' persons by turning asbestos-related disease sufferers into NNS clients and claimants in the Gencor case. This transformation was mediated by four documents which set the terms of the individual registrant's relationship to NNS: (1) a power of attorney and mandate form; (2) a consent form; (3) an agreement concerning fees; and (4) a detailed client questionnaire. We will examine these in turn.

(1) The power of attorney and mandate

The power of attorney and mandate (Figure 5.2) authorized NNS 'to act as my attorneys' and 'to make and prosecute a civil claim on my behalf.' What began in the mass registration drive as a mobilization to recruit potential claimants was reformulated in the power of attorney and mandate as the client's agency in authorizing legal representation. The textual convention is that of the client 'giving instructions' to an attorney, asserting the right of free men and women to employ legal counsel to initiate proceedings on their behalf.

At the same time, however, by signing the power of attorney and mandate, registrants submitted to professional authority, granting NNS 'unfettered discretion' in prosecuting the claim. The 'power of substitution' – for NNS to 'act in my name, place and stead' – delegated the authority to speak on the client's behalf. In the dialectic of agency and submission, by 'giving instructions,' the registrants' expression of agency, freely undertaken and uncoerced, resulted in being acted for, in submitting, under the 'power of substitution' clause, to the judgment of others to act as their legal representatives. It was not that form-made clients *lost* agency so much as they *transferred* it across social locations, from the periphery to the center, *in order to make a claim*, to realize the clients' motives by delegating legal counsel to take Gencor to court.

(2) The consent form

The consent form (Figure 5.3) gave NNS permission to inspect the registrant's medical and work records. The consent form, of course, is an iconic document across the professions, extending aspects of the signee's private life to a delegated expert – a scientist, an ethnographer, a medical doctor, a social worker or, in the Gencor case, an attorney – thereby 'making' the social identities of research subjects, informants, patients, cases and clients. In the context of the Gencor case, the client's consent removed the confidentiality that normally protects personal medical records, enabling them to be discharged to the professional scrutiny of NNS attorneys, to move across documentary fields from the medical to the judicial domain, where they were recoded as legal evidence of unlawful harm.

POWER OF ATTORNEY AND MANDATE

I, the undersigned:

....

presently of:

....

and having the ID/passport number:

....

do hereby mandate and authorize Richard Spoor and, or, the partners of Ntuli, Noble & Spoor, with the power of substitution, as my lawful attorneys and agents and to act in my name, place and stead subject to the recordals, limitations and conditions set out below:

1. I record that while working as a miner or as a result of so working, I/my relative contracted occupational lung disease/diseases ("occupational lung disease").

2. I further record that I believe or have been advised that I/my relative may be entitled to compensation or a greater amount of compensation then I/my relative have been awarded by:

   a) My/my relative's employer/s b) my/my relative's former employers c) the agents of such employers d) their respective employees e) their associated entities f) their successors in title, and/or rights and/or obligations g) the state h) specific funds i) specific insurers j) any other person or entity

that might be responsible to compensate me as a result of occupational lung disease I/my relative contracted.

3. I further record that hereby authorize my attorneys to do everything necessary to prosecute or pursue my claim for compensation or increased compensation against one or more of the entities described above for the occupational lung disease from which I now suffer.

4. I further record that I grant an unfettered discretion to my attorneys to:

   a) prosecute my claim or pursue my claim either as an individual claim and/or

   b) prosecute my claims or pursue my claim as part of a group or class action on behalf of people suffering from occupational lung disease; and/or

Figure 5.2 Ntuli, Noble & Spoor, power of attorney and mandate form

(3) The agreement regarding fees

An agreement regarding fees (Figure 5.4) explained that NNS was taking the case on a 'risk' or contingency basis and 'will be able to recover costs and fees only in the event of … being successful.' NNS agreed to take 15% of any successful court award or settlement agreement, which is a modest fee compared to the 30% or more typically taken by plaintiff

CONSENT

I, the undersigned

Name .... (PLEASE PRINT)
I.D. No. ....

do hereby authorize RICHARD SPOOR and the Partners and Professional Assistants of

NTULI, NOBLE & SPOOR INC

or their duly authorized representatives to inspect and, or, obtain copies of:

1. medical reports;
2. hospital records, including x-rays;
3. employment records; and
4. all and any other documents/records/reports/photographs

which relate to me and, or, my minor children, namely:

1. .... ID No ....
2. .... ID No ....
3. .... ID No ....
4. .... ID No ....

and, or the late .... ID No ....
.... (relationship to the deceased)

Access to such records is required by my attorneys for the purpose of conducting legal proceedings on my/our behalf against my ex-employer/employers and/or any associated company or insurer for damages arising from my occupational related disease.

I further authorize my ex-employer/employers and/or any associated company or insurer, and the Director of the MBOD to make such records as requested available to my attorneys for inspection and copying.

I further authorize my attorneys to give permission to any of the defendants' attorneys to inspect and to copy such medical records and other records, and authorize the MBOD/CCOD, or any other company/institution to make such reports and records available to such attorneys for such purpose.

Signed at .... on this .... day of 2002

....

AS WITNESSES: Claimant's Signature

(1) ....

(2) ....

Figure 5.3 Ntuli, Noble & Spoor, consent form

lawyers in the United States. The modesty of the fee enhanced the NNS's reputation of credibility and good character, of being on the people's side and not in it just for themselves. Moreover, the fee structure reassured the AIG and Moffat about the ethical conduct of the case, confirming what they already knew about Spoor's non-commercial motives.

AGREEMENT REGARDING FEES

MADE AND ENTERED INTO
BETWEEN

NTULI, NOBLE & SPOOR INCORPORATED
35 Hendrick Potgieter Street, Nelspruit 1200
including their successors and assigns
also

....
....
[hereinafter referred to as "the Attorneys"]
and

....
....
[hereinafter referred to as "the Client(s)"]

WHEREAS

The Client(s) has instructed the Attorneys to institute proceedings for damages/loss of support against one or more of the following:

. The Griqualand Exploration and Finance Company Limited
2. Gencor Limited
3. African Chrysotile Asbestos (Pty) Limited
4. Msauli Asbes Limited

AND

The Attorneys will take the matter on a risk basis or contingency basis. That is, they will be able to recover costs and fees only in the event of their being successful.

NOW THEREFORE it is agreed that:

1. The Attorneys shall not be entitled to recover their fees and disbursements from the Client(s) save in the event of success in which case the Attorneys shall be entitled to
receive in settlement of their fees and disbursements, 15% of the capital sum that may be awarded to the Client(s) by any court or in terms of any settlement agreement, as well as such party costs as may be recoverable from the Defendants.

2. No further amounts shall be payable by the clients to the Attorney.

3. This arrangement remains in force whatever the degree of success that is reached, that is regardless of size of the award or settlement amount.

SIGNED and DATED at .... this ...... day of .... 2002.
WITNESSES:

1. ....
SIGNATURE OF CLIENT

2. ....
SIGNATURE OF CLIENT

SIGNED and DATED at .... this ...... day of .... 2002.
WITNESSES:

1. ....
For and on behalf of NTULI, NOBLE & SPOOR INC

2. ....
For and on behalf of NTULI, NOBLE & SPOOR INC

Figure 5.4 Ntuli, Noble & Spoor, fees agreement form

(4) The client questionnaire

The longest of the registration forms was the client questionnaire, which provided crucial documentary evidence for the case, including information about work history, evidence of disease, compensation status, dust levels at work, use of safety equipment, knowledge of asbestos risk and financial loss. The canon of uniformity in document design played an important role in providing the empty blanks for AIG community legal workers to fill in on the questionnaire. In 'exemplar artifacts of bureaucratic knowledge,' Jacob (2007: 253) observes, the design of the document 'must be mobilized to capture and preserve attention.'

The attention captured and preserved by the design of the NNS questionnaire concentrated on obtaining information and identifying documents that could satisfy a delictual claim (from the Latin *dēlinquere*, to be at fault, to violate the public conscience) in the common law. Gencor's mining operations, Spoor proposed to show, met the test of a delictual claim, in which unlawful neglect is determined 'in circumstances where the omission incites moral indignation and offends the legal convictions of the community' (Spoor, 2001a). The 'common law of delict,' as Spoor notes, is meant to serve as 'an essential instrument required to ensure that employers comply with their legal responsibilities' (Spoor, 2001a). Delictual claims, in other words, function not just as the legal grounds, at the level of the individual plaintiff, for the compensation of personal injury. They also serve as socially sanctioned deterrents to prevent employer wrongdoing, warranted by the community's sense of justice and its expectation that employers must provide a duty of care for their employees.

In South African law, a delictual claim depended on establishing five elements: (1) harm to the plaintiff; (2) conduct on the part of the defendant; (3) wrongfulness of the conduct; (4) a causal connection between the conduct and harm; and (5) fault or blameworthiness.[11] The blanks on the questionnaire, as designed according to the canon of uniformity, provided the semiotic space to *entextualize* ex-mineworkers' or surviving family members' stark testimony of suffering and corporate guilt as evidence of these necessary legal elements. (We examine in this section how the design of the questionnaire guided entextualization; in the following section, we look at entextualization in terms of Spoor's composition of the founding affidavit.)

The following testimony from an ex-mineworker's widow Kgakgamatso Gloria Phumo illustrates how the design of the questionnaire drew attention to instances of harm to the claimant and Gefco's wrongful conduct, laying the groundwork for the needed causal link between the company's conduct and the harm to the mineworker. The first section establishes the work record of the widow's husband and why he quit working at Gefco:

GEFCO WORK HISTORY

WHEN DID YOUR HUSBAND WORK FOR GEFCO? HOW LONG DID HE WORK FOR GEFCO?
Her husband worked for GEFCO from 1957–1990.

WHAT DID HE DO THERE? DID HE WORK ABOVE OR UNDERGROUND?
He transported asbestos; he was a driver. He worked above ground.

HOW LONG WERE HIS SHIFTS?
He worked from 6am to 7pm. He worked roughly 12 hour shifts.

WHY DID HE STOP WORKING AT THIS JOB?
He started feeling sick and was unhealthy so he stopped working.

DID GEFCO PAY YOU ANY MONEY WHEN HE STOPPED WORKING?
No.

In another section, Phumo describes the harm that came to her husband when he experienced progressively debilitating symptoms:

ILLNESSES

DID HE SEE A DOCTOR ABOUT HIS SICKNESS?
Yes.

WHERE IS THE DOCTOR LOCATED?
At Batlharos.

DID A DOCTOR TELL HIM WHAT HE HAD?
Yes. He had a cold and chest pain and then the doctor told him that it was from asbestos dust but they didn't do x-rays.

WHEN DID HE START FEELING SICK?
He started feeling sick in 1999. The doctors always gave pills but it never helped. At first, he had chest pain which later went to his legs.

WHEN DID THE SICKNESS START GETTING BAD?
1999 it was very bad.

DID HE SWEAT A LOT AT NIGHT?
Yes. He would get cold and then get a lot of blankets and then get hot.

DID HE COUGH?
Yes. He felt that there was something inside but couldn't get it out.

Finally, two sections document the ex-mineworker's experience of exposure in the workplace, illustrating Gefco's negligent conduct and its differential distribution of risk to white and black mine employees:

PROTECTION AGAINST ASBESTOS

DO YOU REMEMBER HIM WEARING ANY PROTECTIVE GEAR WHEN HE WORKED? WHAT WAS THAT PROTECTIVE GEAR?
No.

DO YOU KNOW IF OTHER WORKERS WORE PROTECTIVE EQUIPMENT?
Yes. Some whites had masks.

DO YOU KNOW WHO GAVE THE PROTECTIVE EQUIPMENT?
NA

WARNINGS ABOUT EXPOSURE

DID YOU KNOW IF GEFCO EVER TOLD YOUR HUSBAND ANYTHING ABOUT ASBESTOS DUST?
No. They never told him anything but he was bothered by the dust.

DID HE GO TO ANY TRAINING SESSIONS?
No.

DID THEY EVER INSTRUCT HIM IN PROTECTIVE EQUIPMENT?
NA

DID GEFCO EVER TELL HIM THAT ASBESTOS COULD MAKE HIM SICK?
No. They never told him that asbestos would make him sick.

WAS HE A MEMBER OF A UNION?
No union.

DID THE UNION EVER TELL HIM ANYTHING ABOUT DUST?
NA

No doubt the most poignant line in the questionnaire contains the modal shift from the hypothetical possibility in the question 'Did Gefco ever tell him asbestos *could* make him sick?' to the undeniable inevitability in the widow's answer: 'They never told him that asbestos *would* make him sick' (italics added). The widow's testimony drew the causal link between Gencor's conduct and the wrongful harm that was caused to her husband, investing her account with the capacity to incite moral indignation, that Gencor's blameworthy behavior had violated widely shared norms of justice.

As may be seen, the refractive pressure of the questionnaire's design turned the widow and her family's lived experience into the needed components of a delictual claim. Under the canon of uniformity, the repeatability of categories on the registration forms reframed and remediated villagers' verbal testimony, transforming the plain speech of ordinary villagers into written legal evidence. And it also created a situation in common among registrants, as an emergent group of people who formed the collective base of the case. In the registration campaign, the unit of insurgent lawfare was mass legal action. The goal was to amalgamate the thousands of individual claims, in light of their common interest, in the founding affidavit against Gencor.

The Founding Affidavit

In South African law, the founding affidavit in a civil case is the statement sworn before a commissioner of oaths setting out the facts in support of an applicant's desired relief from the court. The founding affidavit in the Gencor case listed 'Herman Kubari and Others' as the 'Applicants,' and Gencor, Gefco, Msauli and African Chrysotile Asbestos as the 'Respondents.' Through the 'power of substitution,' Spoor occupied the position of 'I, the undersigned' who 'do hereby make oath and state' the particulars of the case. The Applicants included 12 named individuals whose personal affidavits were attached. These were claimants Spoor had assembled by sifting through the registration questionnaires to find the 'right combination' to serve as the public face of the case. The 13th Applicant, as already noted, was the AIG, represented by Stephen Kotoloane's affidavit. From the 14th Applicant on into the thousands were 'persons … too lengthy to be said forth,' the masses of people registered by AIG community legal workers 'who have either contracted an asbestos related disease (an ARD) or who are at substantial risk of contracting same.' The names and details of these Applicants were listed on an attached schedule. For all these people, Spoor was 'duly authorized to depose to this affidavit on their behalf,' to establish before the court the scope of Gencor's wrongdoing, supported by extensive documentary evidence of harm, unlawful conduct and their causal connection.

The two modalities of the AIG/NNS alliance – the grassroots registration drive on the periphery and professional practice in the metropolitan legal sector – intermingled in the founding affidavit. In addition to the 13 personal affidavits, the founding affidavit contained 'research by suitably qualified experts into various aspects relating to the merits and quantum of the claims. These experts include – medical specialists, occupational health specialists, epidemiologists, actuaries, scientists and historians.' Part of the research incorporated into the founding affidavit was a literature review of the 'major developments of medical knowledge about asbestos' from 1898 to 1962, to demonstrate that the 'harmful effects of asbestos are well known and recognized for a great many years' and thereby to show the wrongfulness of Gencor's conduct in ignoring the admitted dangers of asbestos. The founding affidavit also included a timeline of Gencor's involvement in asbestos mining and an overview, based on its annual financial reports, that established Gencor's ownership of Gefco, Msauli and African Chrysotile and its consequent legal responsibility for their operations. In addition, Spoor managed to obtain reports of dust levels and air quality control from the Department of Minerals and Energy, comprising 15,000 pages of documents which, as Spoor notes in the founding affidavit to block Gencor's unbundling, have only begun to be examined. The mass of documentary evidence in the founding affidavit grew to over 6000 pages, organized in 14 volumes. As we will see, in the agonistic arena of the law, the sheer volume of documentary evidence on the part of the plaintiff is meant to exert an epistemic force on the defendant, as more evidence than can possibly be refuted, thereby applying a pressure to settle without going to court.

Documentary evidence drawn from elite sectors was also at times woven into the verbal testimony of the 13 individual Applicants, as is evident in the lead affidavit of Herman Kubari. To make the causal link between employer conduct and wrongful injury, Kubari's affidavit begins by recounting the conditions at the Riries mine where he worked as a crusher operator:

> 4. I was employed by Gefco at Riries mine as a crusher: my duties entailed the following:
>   4.1. To push asbestos stones with bare hands and feet into the crusher machine which was situated at the plant. The rubber coverage of the crusher machine which was supposed to prevent asbestos dust from emanating from the crusher machine itself was defective for the whole period I was there. Consequently, my co-workers and I had to cover the rubber cover with our hands in an attempt to avoid asbestos dust escaping into our work environment.
>   4.2. I had to remove asbestos filled bags from the crusher machine at a tremendous pace to keep up with the filling process. The bags were thereafter removed. We had to sew the bags shut with needle and thread.
>   4.3. During these procedures we were exposed to great volumes of asbestos dust. Our hair, clothes and faces were covered with vast quantities of asbestos dust.
>   4.4. We noticed the foremen wore masks to cover their noses and mouths, but we were too afraid to ask the purpose and accepted matters as such.
>   4.5. We worked 12 hour-day shifts. We were 12 in a team who worked at the crushing machine.
>   4.6. At the end of the working day our faces, hair and clothes were habitually covered with asbestos dust and no shower facilities were supplied at the mine.

A few sections later, Kubari's affidavit describes the onset of illness:

> 6. Toward the end of my employment at Riries mine, I started to feel ill. My nose started to bleed and I started coughing. I decided to resign. I visited Dr. Grobler at Kuruman, who gave me cough syrup.

Kubari had fluid and blood drained from his lungs four times in 2000. In 2002 Kubari went to the Klerksdorp Hospital where he was biopsied. He stayed in the hospital for three weeks, but when he received 'no specialized treatment,' he 'insisted to be discharged.'

At this point, Kubari's personal testimony is interrupted and the register of the affidavit shifts dramatically as a radiological report from the Klerksdorp Hospital, dated 16 July 2002, is inserted into the document in quotes to indicate the passage is being moved from its original context, as a 'secondary source' distinguished from Kubari's verbal testimony as the primary source:

> 'Lobulated soft tissue masses are seen extending throughout the left pleural space. There is associated collapse of the underlying left lung. Note that the pleural masses extending along the mediastinal pleura and there is strong suspicion of infiltration of tumour into the medistatinum. It is difficult separating tumour tissue from descending thoracic aorta. Generally there is a plane of cleavage between the heart and the tumour but, in places, there is strong suspicion of infiltration of the pericardium. There is loss of definition of the left diaphragmatic crus raising suspicion of early infiltration into the abdominal cavity'.
>
> 'Post contrast film show moderate peripheral enhancement of tumour with central areas of low attenuation suggesting necrosis. There is also an encysted pleural collection in the left lower zone'.
>
> 'Comment: The appearances are of advanced mesothelioma'.

It is uncertain why Kubari did not receive treatment at Klerksdorp, but in any event he returns in the affidavit to Dr Grobler, who referred him to the Kuruman Hospital, which then sent him to the Kimberley Hospital for another biopsy. These wanderings through the medical system – the neglect and wasted time – are painful to read. Mesothelioma was confirmed, and as Kubari's affidavit says:

> 11. Currently I am still receiving chemotherapy and get painkillers for the immense pain I am suffering. This therapy I am receiving makes me tremendously ill. So much that I have to stay at home for long periods of time, during which I receive no remuneration.

Herman Kubari died on 25 January 2003. In a special arrangement, he received compensation before the Gencor settlement in March of that year.

The rhetorical power of Kubari's personal affidavit comes in part from the plain style of his verbal testimony and in part from how his private suffering is confirmed by the impersonal and technical style of medical diagnosis, as the metropolitan authority of specialist knowledge serves to warrant the ordinary speech of personal experience. This combination of offsetting discourses, moreover, underscores the composed character of the individual affidavits. They are not simply transcripts of speech, presented as a literal record of what was spoken. Rather they *entextualize* the verbal testimony (and sometimes, as in Kubari's case, other documents) in a particular genre of legal writing, the affidavit.

As Greg Urban notes, the term *entextualization* refers to 'the process of rendering a particular instance of discourse a text, detachable from its local context' (Urban, 1996: 21). The notion of entextualization, in this regard, helps explain how discourse-rendered-as-text can become portable and mobile, able to move from its place of origin and be inserted into other texts and contexts. Spoor's entextualization of Kubari's verbal testimony shows, for example, how spoken discourse can be mixed with texts from quite different social locations (such as Kubari's medical diagnosis), retrofitted to new contexts of use and meaning by professional practice. As Urban notes further, when entextualization involves replication (when Spoor, for example, renders clients' speech as the verbal testimony of the affidavit), the relation of 'original' and 'copy' inevitably poses the question of the asymmetrical distribution of rhetorical agency.

Spoor's rendering of Kubari's testimony was itself enabled by a chain of prior documents, in particular the power of attorney and mandate that delegated to Spoor the 'power of substitution,' with its authority to speak on behalf of his clients. We have already seen in the mass registration drive of the Gencor case how the dialectic of agency and submission played itself out in the fashioning of 'form-made persons,' as asbestos-related disease sufferers were transformed into clients and claimants by 'giving instructions' that delegated to NNS the authority to act in their interest. Here we look at the dynamics of agency and submission at the point of production, to examine how a lawyer's authorship of verbal testimony remediates the claimant's spoken discourse, transforming it into a written affidavit.

The legal significance of verbal testimony sworn under oath is that it is treated as truthfully spoken, as a factual account unless disputed. Its spoken character invests the affidavit with an aura of authenticity and truth telling that comes from the eye-witness authority of personal experience – as something that really happened to a person and therefore can reliably be believed. As Spoor noted retrospectively, composing the affidavits was in part an act of ventriloquism, of trying to capture the speaking voice of the individual. This is evident, for example, in the plain-spoken register of Kubari's testimony, rendered as the everyday speech of an ordinary worker, and how it creates an ethos of honesty, straightforwardness and the credibility of first-hand experience. And yet, as Spoor further acknowledged, composing the individual affidavits was also inevitably the act of a 'specialist in litigation,' a textual representation of the plaintiff that sought on the one hand to evoke the sound of the person's voice, but on the other was designed to speak on the person's behalf, 'to articulate the circumstances,' Spoor said, 'better than the person can do.'[12] In this sense, the truthfulness of verbal testimony as it appears in individual affidavits like Kubari's does not only derive from its fidelity to what the plaintiff actually said but is also a matter of rhetorical artifice – not a deception but the technê of making prior statements (the 'original') count as a certain kind of truth (the 'copy'), recognized as legal evidence.

A similar process may be observed in the affidavit of Gloria Phumo (one of the 13 individual affidavits in the founding legal documents) whose client questionnaire we examined earlier. The brief note at the end of the questionnaire that she was having a difficult time supporting her family is amplified in her verbal testimony. She recounts the events surrounding the illness and death of her husband, who never received any compensation and whose cause of death was listed on the death certificate as 'dyspnea chest pain' but almost certainly was mesothelioma. The trials of the widow's family, first recorded in passing on the client questionnaire, reappears in the affidavit as a causal sequence of immiseration, as the husband's illness and death plunges the family further and further into poverty and suffering. As Phumo says concerning her husband's illness, 'Due to the state he was in, I had to nurse him, wash him, feed him, and clothe him,' revealing the invisible uncompensated labor of family members who absorbed the burden of caring for asbestos-related disease sufferers and then are left with no provisions for the future.

The individual affidavit goes on to explain the consequences of her husband's death:

> 16. Due to my own medical condition, (I am an epileptic sufferer), I am unable to do work to support my family.
> 17. I have two young children who were dependant on my husband's income and as a result we were forced to sell our house at Sedibeng in order to be closer to Tshwaragano Hospital where my husband received treatment. The money that was generated through the sale of our house, had to be spent on school fees, medical expenses, traveling and food. We now live in a shanty house which consists of only one room that is built with corrugated iron. We are totally dependant on my widowed sister, who is also a pensioner and sometimes provides us with the bare necessities. My children who are still in school are forced to go without food on most occasions.
> 18. Due to my husband's illness he was unable to make provisions for our present and future needs which resulted that my children and I are left destitute.

The numbered sections move with an implacable narrative force but they also interrupt and fragment the narrative, turning the widow's testimony visually into individual units of documentary evidence. Just as the AIG's grassroots maps were remediated in Robert Jones' scientific studies and David Goldblatt's photographs, the widow's testimony undergoes a passage of form, a rhetorical transformation that reorganizes the flow of speech, breaking it up and recontextualizing it according to the textual conventions of the affidavit.

As Michael Silverstein and Greg Urban (1996: 4) write, 'entextualization both reflects and constitutes asymmetrical social relations'. Such a view, of course, helps make sense of lawyer–client relations, with their power of substitution and delegation of authority. We must be careful, however, not to see the case of the legal affidavit as simply the replacement of an 'original' with a 'copy,' whereby Kubari's or Phumo's speaking voice is the originating source, which is then appropriated secondarily through the exercise of professional power and rendered as text. We must acknowledge that the composition of affidavits is not unidirectional (the client's words transformed by the lawyer) but bidirectional (running as well in the other direction from text to discourse).

The special authority invested legally in verbal testimony derives not just from its originality (coming directly from the first-hand experience of the plaintiff) or its 'naturalness' as speech (before the artifice of writing) but rather from its position in a network of texts, including: the oath sworn before the court, which authorizes the inclusion of the testimony in the legal record; the power of attorney and mandate that delegates the power of substitution to the lawyer; and the generally accepted textual conventions of the affidavit as a well-known, highly formulaic genre of legal writing. There is a sense in which the originating discourse – Kubari's or Phumo's spoken account – is *already* framed as text. The lateral diffusion of rhetorical agency that occurs when Kubari and Phumo speak under oath ends up being concentrated vertically in the rhetorical agency of the lawyer, as Spoor recontextualizes Kubari's and Phumo's spoken words as verbal testimony in a written affidavit. These are the prestructured realities – and rhetorical transformations – of lawyer–client relations. They are not, as Jacobs says, a 'zero-sum' game but they are not exactly symmetrical either.

The Settlement

In the founding affidavit to block the Gencor unbundling, Spoor notes that in 'the time available to us we have barely begun to record and collate the mass of verbal testimony from [Gencor] ex-employees ... including geologists, engineers, mine managers and even past directors of the company who have indicated a willingness to consult with us.' It is hard to miss here the gamesmanship of insurgent lawfare – and the wry pleasure Spoor must have felt – in hinting that he possessed a mass of incriminating testimony from Gencor insiders that he had only begun to analyze. The point of the founding affidavit was to provide overwhelming evidence from multiple spheres – the massive number of claimants, the volume of documentary evidence already assembled and the veiled threat of worse to come. Its rhetorical force was to dissuade Gencor attorneys from going to court, to persuade them they would have no chance trying the case but would be better off agreeing to an out-of-court settlement.

This, of course, is exactly what happened, and the founding affidavit was never adjudicated before the law and Spoor's legal reasoning was never tested. The NNS motion to interdict Gencor's unbundling was heard in the High Court in Johannesburg between 19 and 22 November 2002, with a ruling promised for January 2003. By that time, however, Gencor was already negotiating a settlement, and the case never reached a legal conclusion. An out-of-court settlement was signed on 13 March 2003, creating, as we will see in the next chapter, the Asbestos Relief Trust (ART) and a new political economy of certifiable asbestos-related disease.

In the end, the founding affidavit was filed away, entering the vast uncharted domain of untried legal cases. Still, the verbal testimony of the 13 Applicants (the 12 named individuals plus the AIG) lingers in file drawers as eloquent, formerly unheard voices mobilized by grassroots activism, their individual affidavits giving powerful witness to the suffering of ex-mineworkers and their families and to Gencor's corporate crimes.

Notes

(1) On Concerned People Against Asbestos (CPAA), see McCulloch (2005b) and Waldman (2007, 2011: 53–60, 113–114).

(2) This discussion of the Cape plc legal case draws on Falender (2002), McCulloch (2005b) and Spoor (2001a).

(3) Before the Cape plc case, Leigh, Day & Co. had attempted twice to establish the standing of Southern African workers to sue in British courts. In the first instance, a 1995 case discovered compelling evidence of the negligent mercury poisoning of workers at Thor Chemical's Cato Ridge plant in Natal but was settled out of court, and the question of legal forum was never adjudicated. The second case, representing a worker who developed throat cancer at RTZ's Rossing uranium mine in Namibia, was thrown out in 1998 by the statute of limitations, again taking the issue of forum off the judicial agenda.

(4) Cape achieved significant concessions. For one, the documents involved in the settlement were destroyed. In addition, Cape was absolved of any responsibility for rehabilitating its former mines and dumps, passing on the costs to the new South African government. Earlier, in January 2001, Richard Spoor wrote to Enver Daniels, the Chief Law Advisor in the UK, warning that, with the settlement of the Cape case near at hand, there needed to be close attention to keeping Cape from evading its responsibility for rehabilitation.

(5) Linda Waldman contrasts the 'relative isolation experienced by Griquatown residents with the networking and mobilisation process taking place in Prieska' to explain the more negative reactions in Griquatown, where 'this isolation undermines citizens' ability to frame asbestos disease litigation as an international victory and as a case of justice being done' (Waldman, 2007: iii).

(6) These papers include Spoor (2001a, 2001b, 2003a, 2003b).

(7) Spoor foresaw that such a scale would require extensive resources far beyond NNS means. He reached an understanding with London-based Thompson Solicitors, a labor law firm with a long record of representing British asbestos workers, which agreed to fund the case and provide legal assistance. Thompsons paid for two lawyers: Spoor, who worked out of the NNS office in Nelspruit, and an attorney located in Kuruman.

(8) Richard Aitken used the term 'institutional virtue' in a letter to me of 9 February 2016, recalling the role of Moffat Mission in the Gencor case. Noting the 'entire edifice of an ecclesiastical authority standing behind' Moffat, Aitken wrote: 'It was precisely that institutional virtue that we had called upon to underwrite our capacity to insulate the participant asbestos claimants from legal abuse, or at least the hypothesis of abuse that seemed to hang in the air for so many.'

(9) Richard Aitken to Right Reverend Itumeleng Moseki, 10 October 2002.

(10) Brenda Sethibeng, interview by Lundy Braun, 21 September 2003.

(11) As normative elements, 'wrongful' means a failure of conduct, for example, that an employer should have known better or taken steps to prevent injury or disease, while 'fault' refers to the degree to which wrongful conduct offends the public conscience.

(12) Richard Spoor, discussion with author, 20 August 2015.

6 'The Lawyer Stole the Money': The Political Economy of Certifiable Asbestos-related Disease

On 16 June 2010 – Youth Day in South Africa, the national holiday that celebrates the 1976 student uprising in Soweto – Julius Malema, who was then chairman of the ANC Youth League, addressed an overflow crowd at Bathlaros Stadium, about half an hour's drive from Kuruman. The event was sponsored by the Asbestos Kgatelopele Community (AKC), a local group from Maruping that had broken with the AIG to set itself up as the authentic grassroots opposition in the Kuruman district to the Asbestos Relief Trust (ART). At the center of Malema's speech was the rumor being circulated by the AKC that Richard Spoor had stolen the ART money and that was why sick people with asbestos-related diseases were not receiving compensation. As Malema informed his listeners:

> Comrades I am glad to announce that last night we managed to get the contacts of that Mr. Spoorman who stole your money. We searched for him until we found out that he is hiding somewhere in Pretoria, we are going to make sure that he comes back to Maruping and brings back your money. (Leburu, 2010: 2)

This farfetched tale about Spoor fit into in an older pattern of rumors about imaginary sums of money 'from overseas' that were somehow blocked or stolen, kept from villagers by shadowy forces – rumors that tapped into a long history of desperate poverty, social abandonment and unmet promises (AC, 2001: 65). Malema's appearance on behalf of the AKC was meant to turn these longstanding feelings of deception and betrayal against the ART and its AIG ally.

By 2010, discontent with the ART was stirring in the villages. The great expectations released by the founding of the ART in 2003 – the promise of relief from the disaster of life in the former asbestos mining districts – had faded, as the inexorable logic of the trust's eligibility standards for compensation unfolded at the grassroots level. Everyone knew someone or had heard about someone whose claim had been rejected but who was just as sick and needy as those who got compensation. There was talk, moreover, that some people received compensation money but did not deserve it, or that trust officials were hoarding the money or spending it on themselves. Disappointment with the ART created fertile ground at the grassroots level for rumors like 'the lawyer stole the money.'

The point of this chapter is to examine the aftermath of the Gencor settlement and the dilemmas of the payout-for-personal-injury model of compensation in post-liberation South Africa. With the establishment in 2003 of the ART – and then in 2006 the smaller Kgalagadi Relief Trust (KRT), following an out-of-court settlement with the Swiss asbestos giant Eternit – the AIG's situation and the nature of its work changed. For one thing, shortly after the Gencor settlement, the AIG's alliance with Moffat ended and the AIG left the mission, setting up an office in Kuruman and registering with the state as an independent nonprofit organization. In addition, the coming of the ART and KRT meant the focus of the AIG's textual labor shifted from the legal front of registering claimants in the Gencor and Eternit cases to helping villagers assemble the paperwork needed to file compensation claims with the trusts or the state system. Most of all, the AIG found itself at a new point in its history, entangled in the uses and limits of the trusts and the state compensation system, confronting daily how the promise of compensation played out unevenly in the lives of villagers in the Kuruman district. As we will see, the AIG was tested in the post-settlement years by circumstances no-one could have foretold when the Gencor case ended in 2003.

The Political Economy of Compensation

The earliest known workers' compensation systems are found in ancient Sumeria. The Nippur Tablet No. 3191, *c.*2050 BCE, contains the law of Ur-Nammu, King of Ur, which provided monetary compensation for personal injuries such as fractures or loss of limbs. The Code of Hammurabi, from 1750 BCE, included what amounts to a catalog of body parts, listing the different payments for the loss of a hand, an eye, a leg, and so on. Similar systems appear in ancient Greek, Roman and Arabic law, setting the monetary value of death or personal injury. In its early forms, compensation was usually calculated in terms of *impairment*, or the physical capacity the worker lost or had damaged. This way of reckoning value differs from (but is also a precursor to) the idea of *disability* in modern industrial-age state compensation systems, where the locus of value shifts from lost life and limbs to wages lost due to the inability to work. By the early 20th century, state compensation systems began to recognize occupational disease, as well as workplace injuries, as grounds for compensation (Guyton, 1999).

Compensation systems monetize the burden of risk by creating schedules that cross-reference various types of work-related disease and injury to their respective monetary values. The act of scheduling compensation recognizes – and implicitly accepts the fact – that risk is an inevitable part of work, bound to occur under the prevailing conditions of production, whether due to accident, hazardous materials, faulty machinery, employer neglect or some other cause or combination of causes. Compensation systems are designed to deflect potentially subversive questions about responsibility for health and safety in the workplace by prefiguring risk, quantifying it into knowable entities, making death and injury routine and official, inscribed in schedules that replace irreplaceable loss with monetary equivalences.

Compensation schedules often use tables to represent the moral, legal and economic equivalence of personal injury and money. As a graphic design, the tabular form makes physical loss and the amount of payment allotted to it appear as interchangeable measures of value, organized in predictably ordered rows and columns of recognition (the injury) and restitution (the payment). This is evident, for example, in the ART's compensation schedule which divides the four asbestos-related diseases recognized by the trust – pleural thickening, asbestosis, asbestos-related lung cancer and mesothelioma – into levels of severity, with corresponding increases in the amount of compensation, as may be seen in Figure 6.1.

Compensation schedules are semiotic devices meant to *contain* the burden of risk at work, in the double sense of *representing* risk graphically, as something that can be predicted and displayed in the typographic space of the page, and *absorbing* risk's convulsive materializations and meanings in workers' lives. By assigning a price, through the payout of claims, compensation schedules are designed to contain the threat of personal vengeance or other forms of popular non-state sanctioned justice, to halt blame for the causes of death and injury and eliminate any further recourse to action. In the unfolding sequence, compensation figures as the

Compensation categories & amounts	4 categories – ARDs 1, 2, 3 & 4
ARD 1 ~ R38,000	Asbestos related pleural thickening and/or asbestosis, with mild or moderate lung function loss
ARD 2 ~ R78,000	Asbestos related pleural thickening and/or asbestosis, with severe lung function loss
ARD 3 ~ R174,000	Asbestos related lung cancer
ARD 4 ~ R349,000	Mesothelioma (Pleural or peritoneal cancer)

Figure 6.1 Asbestos Relief Trust, compensation schedule

moment of closure when matters are settled, questions are dropped and the people injured sign off in exchange for the cash benefit.

The *Deed of Trust Creating the Asbestos Relief Trust* (hereafter, Trust Deed) charged the ART with setting up a private, legally sanctioned compensation system that carried out functions normally performed by the state, such as determining eligibility for compensation, processing claims and administering benefits.[1] The Trust Deed gave the newly established ART and its board of five trustees[2] broad discretion in devising the 'administrative mechanisms' needed to fulfill the terms of the Gencor settlement. To do this, the ART established the paperwork needed to certify claimants' eligibility for compensation according to the dual criteria established by the Trust Deed: (1) 'reasonable proof' of the claimant's exposure working on or living near mines and mills owned by the founders of the ART, based on work records or proof of residency; and (2) a diagnosis certified by an expert medical panel of asbestos-related disease, based on clinical examination, x-rays, the use of spirometers to measure lung function, biopsies and other standard medical procedures. The Trust Deed spelled out, in effect, the kind of documentation needed to verify a claim. The ART, for its part, created the bureaucratic apparatus to connect the various medical, legal and work records needed to file and process claims.

The ART's bureaucratic apparatus consisted in large part of professional services outsourced to perform necessary functions in the paperwork of the trust's operations. These included:

- actuarial experts who determined the quantum of awards;
- physicians in Kuruman and elsewhere who conducted medical examinations;
- the expert medical panel at the University of Cape Town Lung Institute who read the medical findings to determine whether claimants were entitled to compensation and to what degree;
- the team from Canon who digitized over 810,000 Gefco and Msauli work records;
- the IT specialists who developed customized software for the trust; and
- the claims handlers who helped villagers assemble records and fill out the paperwork needed to file a claim.[3]

The bureaucratic apparatus that the ART set up to manage the paperwork of a private compensation system infused small amounts of new capital into the South African economy, creating its own mini-political economy in order to carry out the terms of the Gencor settlement. We will see shortly how this political economy affected the AIG, especially in regard to the claims-handling sector of the trust's operation. The point to emphasize at the outset, however, is that the central commodity brought into being by the ART's upstart economy was certifiable asbestos-related disease. Accordingly, the first task of the trust was to monetize disease, to create exchange values for the burden of risk imposed on mineworkers and the general population living in the vicinity of asbestos mines and mills without their knowledge. The Trust Deed gave the ART six months to set up a formula of benefits, during which time no awards, with a few exceptions, were made.[4]

As J.M. teWaterNaude points out, the Gencor settlement differed from the Cape plc case, in which all 7500 individuals listed as litigants were compensated (Naude, 2014: 4–5). The Gencor settlement, in contrast, was open ended, with the anticipation that over a 25-year operation the trust would compensate future claimants who had not yet developed asbestos-related disease, given its long incubation span. Compared to the set list of beneficiaries in the Cape case, at the time of the Gencor settlement the number of successful claims to be expected was not yet determined.

The trust turned to the health care actuary Greg Smith, of Fifth Quadrant Actuaries and Consultants, to do the following: (1) to estimate the number of claims that would be registered over the 25-year life of the ART and, of this total, how many would be certified for compensation; and (2) based on these projections, to set the amount of individual benefits, taking into consideration pain and suffering, loss of wages and medical expenses incurred by qualifying claimants. Smith drew on published scientific findings as well as some commissioned work to estimate that: 16,800 individuals would register claims with the trust; 5036 (later raised to 5162) claims would be certified; and, of the qualifying claimants, approximately 3% would have lung cancer, approximately 11% mesothelioma and the rest – well over 80% – would have impaired lung function, although Smith did not predict the ratio of ARD 1 and ARD 2. As it turned out, Smith's estimates were on target, as may be seen in the total of more than 16,000 claims the ART had processed by 2014, of which 5400 or approximately 30% were certified as compensable asbestos related disease (BizNews, 2014).

At first glance the 30% certification rate of claimants may seem low and disappointing, somehow letting many needs and much suffering go unaddressed. What must be understood, however, is that if the ART did a thorough job of screening potentially eligible claimants – which, to its great credit, it did do through active outreach, in part with the AIG, in the former asbestos mining districts in South Africa and in labor-sending regions in Lesotho, Swaziland, Botswana and elsewhere – the number of qualifying claims would end up around 30%, or roughly equivalent to the incidence of asbestos-related disease found in the available epidemiological studies. In other words, it was because of the scope of the screening – growing out of the ART's desire for eligible ex-mineworkers not to fall through the cracks – that only 30% qualified for compensation.

The scientific underpinnings of Smith's actuarial projections gave epistemic authority to the ART's 30% compensation rate, verifying its accuracy and confirming the conscientiousness and validity of the ART's methods according to metropolitan standards. At the grassroots level, however, the popular understanding of the trust's 30% certification rate was uneven at best. Instead, the Gencor settlement figured initially in popular consciousness as a fulfillment of justice that held the asbestos industry accountable for the disaster it had created. The Setswana term *puna kaledi*, or 'sorry money,' evoked a historic sense of restitution whereby villagers would at last be paid for their pain and suffering.

Popular sentiments in the Kuruman district were similar in many respects to what Adriana Petryna found in the aftermath of the 1986 Chernobyl nuclear disaster, in another place where land and life had been devastated by environmental catastrophe. The grassroots forces mobilized in the insurgent lawfare of the Gencor case shared with Chernobyl survivors a demand for what, in the face of such disasters to life, Petryna calls 'biological citizenship' – the right to biomedical resources, a safe environment and restitution. In South Africa, where the black rural working class had long been disenfranchised subjects of white minority rule, the prospects of citizenship in the post-liberation polity intensified feelings that villagers had a right to the protection of life guaranteed in the new constitution and reparations for years of injury and neglect.

And yet, as Petryna (2002: 6, italics added) notes, there is a tension between the '*massive demand for* but *selective access to* a form of social welfare based on medical, scientific, and legal criteria that both acknowledge biological injury and compensate for it.' In the case of the ART, villagers' needs vastly exceeded the terms of eligibility set legally by the Trust Deed. Epistemic differences separated the ART's administration of *selective access* to compensation – based on the professional expertise of actuarial estimates of medical diagnosis and on the legal conditions of the out-of-court settlements that limited compensation to the mines owned by Gencor and Eternit – from the *massive demand* for biological citizenship and the protection of life in post-liberation South Africa. The 'sorry money' of the popular imagination envisaged reparations as the redistribution of the asbestos industry's ill-gotten gains, made available to all who have suffered from living and working in the former asbestos mining districts.

This emphasis on popular justice put villagers in an uneasy relationship with the 'medical, scientific, and legal criteria' according to which the ART operated, the epistemic regimes of professional expertise (such as actuarial science, biomedical research, clinical diagnosis, trust administration, legal counsel, and so on) that animated the workings of the ART. As Kotoloane and Aitken had worried, villagers' hopes exceeded any realistic outcome that might follow from a settlement with Gencor or Eternit. Shattered expectations and feelings of betrayal materialized as villagers became aware of how the paperwork of the trust sorted the general suffering into categories of eligibility and ineligibility, allotting benefits to roughly one-third of claimants while withholding them from others who were just as poor and needy.

As we will see in a moment, this tension between demand and access – the call for biological citizenship straining against the legal limits of the Trust Deed – shaped the daily encounters of the AIG with villagers and with the political opposition to the ART during the post-settlement period in Kuruman. First, however, we must follow the AIG in the years immediately after the Gencor legal campaign, when it was caught up in struggles over paperwork that occurred in the claims-handling sector of the political economy of certifiable asbestos-related disease.

The AIG and Paperwork Struggles in the Claims-handling Sector

At the time when Richard Aitken left Moffat Mission in 2003, the Gencor case had just been settled. Reverend Larry R. Colvin, the head of the Kalahari Desert School of Theology, took over Aitken's former position as director of the Kuruman Moffat Mission Trust. In a fateful move, Colvin allied himself at the mission with Reza Williams, the husband of Feirouz Williams, the lawyer hired to represent Ntuli, Noble & Spoor (NNS) and work with the ART in Kuruman. Reza Williams was hired initially as a consultant and then became the manager of the Maphakela Centre at Moffat, where he quickly developed a working relationship with Colvin.

This partnership, which was to have unsettling effects on the AIG, was shaped by a specific conjuncture in Kuruman following the Gencor settlement, when the new economy of certifiable asbestos-related disease created by the ART converged with the ANC's turn at the national level to the entrepreneurialism of free-market economics. In a dramatic and controversial development, the ANC shifted from the radical populism of the 1955 Freedom Charter – with its commitments to nationalizing key sectors of the economy, undoing the social and economic inequality inherited from years of apartheid, segregation and colonialism, and promoting a popular participatory democracy – to the neoliberal orientation of the 1996 Growth, Employment and Redistribution platform (GEAR).[5] A tonal shift occurred in South Africa as a new business mentality began to replace the consciousness-raising spirit of the struggle years. The watchwords became 'economic freedom' and 'economic empowerment,' making it socially acceptable, as part of the ANC's plan for national prosperity, to be an entrepreneur in the black economic empowerment schemes of the corporate sector and in the tender capitalism that ransacked the state treasury.

In tune with GEAR's market mentality, the Williams-Colvin leadership considered ways to leverage the mission's assets, to capitalize on Moffat Mission as a heritage site in South Africa's tourism economy rather than as an outpost of the new democratic public sphere, which had been the vision of the AIG/Moffat alliance. Little came of plans to build a swimming pool, upgrade accommodations at the Maphakela Centre or link up with the small private game reserve across the highway from the mission. More ominous was the fact that, as Stephen Kotoloane noted, Williams and Colvin quickly became aware of the AIG's funding capacity, including the R100,000 it had received from the financial services conglomerate SANLAM, the ART and other donors. Under the terms of the constitution, the AIG's funds were held by Moffat as the fiscal agent.[6] Following Aitken's departure, the external funding he had secured from foundations and charitable philanthropies for community-based projects at Moffat dried up, shrinking the financial resources of the mission. Williams and Colvin had no interest in continuing Aitken's grassroots activism, and they turned instead to the new political economy of certifiable asbestos-related disease established by the Gencor settlement, projecting a role for the mission in the claims-handling sector.

As was true with the other professional services it outsourced, the ART did not have the personnel or the infrastructure to assist all individuals in putting together the necessary paperwork to file a claim, given the volume being registered. The ART's claims-handling policy took time to work out, and in the earliest days of the trust, before procedures were fully in place, there was a certain boom-town mentality at Moffat Mission, fueled by the ANC's new entrepreneurial spirit, about the prospects of a freewheeling for-profit claims-handling economy created by ART's outsourcing. As the ART was working out a viable policy about who would be approved to handle claims and how fees would be set, Williams and Colvin formed a claims-handling operation at the mission, the Moffat Asbestos Alliance (MAA), with the AIG providing fieldworkers to recruit potential claimants, serve as translators and lend popular legitimacy to the enterprise.

It is worth noting that Moffat could have set up a nonprofit claims-handling service with funding from the ART or elsewhere to cover staff and overheads. Such an initiative would have been very much in line with the grassroots activism of the AIG/Moffat alliance during Aitken's directorship. Instead of seeing claims handling as a service to the community, however, Williams and Colvin conceived of the MAA as a moneymaking opportunity. From the ART's side, by paying for each claim submitted, the trust hoped to provide financial incentives to screen as widely as possible – a proactive approach to identifying potentially eligible claimants that highlighted the integrity of the ART in carrying out the terms of the Trust Deed. Nonetheless, despite these good intentions, by monetizing each claim handled the ART inadvertently encouraged MAA's market mentality, in which profit came from the volume of claims produced, with quality control as a secondary consideration.

The potential conflict lurking between the ART's desire to screen as widely as possible and the MAA's profit-driven operations quickly came to a head. The result was an ongoing paperwork struggle between the ART and MAA, a struggle over the MAA's access to the paperwork of claims handling as a newly available profit center in the political economy of certifiable asbestos-related disease. In May 2004, when the MAA submitted over 200 claims – some of which were incomplete – the ART agreed to pay over R1000 per claim, but decided to stop accepting claims from the MAA.

This step by the ART, however, did not end the struggle between the trust and mission forces over access to the paperwork of claims handling. After the MAA terminated operations, Williams set up Moffat Asbestos Claims Handlers (MACH) as an independent operation, with an office in Kuruman, that used the mission's name and a silhouette of Robert Moffat on its logo to extend the semiotic authority of the mission to MACH. Williams also took with him some of the leading AIG activists who had been part of MAA. When the ART objected to Williams being the manager of MACH as a conflict of interest, since his wife was involved in trust affairs, Itumeleng Sithole replaced Williams as the titular MACH manager, although Williams continued to be involved behind the scenes.

In any case, at Williams' initiative, the MAA proceeded to form a partnership with a local doctor. Since the ART paid for medical examinations of claimants as well as for claims handling, this was a potent profit-making combine to take into the villages, to do medical screenings with a portable x-ray machine and register claimants. It was also, at least in theory, a good idea for such mobile units to operate on behalf of the ART and its goal of screening as widely as possible. The problem, however, was the quality of the x-rays produced by the portable machine. This became an issue when the ART was forced to reject MACH x-rays because they were unreadable or just marginally readable but insufficient for diagnostic purposes. The MACH x-rays' lack of legibility meant, in effect, that they were non-exchangeable – they could not be monetized – in the claims-handling economy of the trust. The paperwork struggle between the trust and mission forces effectively ended when MACH x-rays were disqualified. By 2006 the ART was no longer accepting claims from MACH, and the enterprise dissolved.

As the paperwork struggles of the ART and the mission unfolded, the MAA and MACH's entrepreneurial market-oriented approach to claims handling put the AIG in a difficult position. On the one hand, the Williams-Colvin leadership needed the AIG, as translators and community representatives, to give MACH access to potential claimants. On the other hand, the Moffat leadership was trying at the same time to gain greater control of the AIG as part of its claims-handling workforce by defining the AIG as a department of the mission instead of an independent village-based organization in an alliance with the mission. This meant treating AIG coordinator Stephen Kotoloane as a subordinate who, according to his terms of employment in the AIG constitution, reported to and required permission from the Moffat director Colvin to carry out AIG activities.

The new political alignment at the mission posed a sharp risk, Kotoloane recalled, to the AIG's standing in the villages and its reputation in the NGO sector. There were the dangers, he noted, of being overly identified with Moffat, as the mission's community programs fell apart, and of being aligned with its claims-handling wing, given its mercenary interests and the problematic character of its work. During this time of crisis in the early post-settlement period, Kotoloane says, it felt like Williams and Colvin were trying to split the AIG, luring some to work for MACH, while restricting the AIG's capacity as a grassroots organization to act on its own. Kotoloane and the AIG executive committee quietly began to explore the possibilities of rewriting the constitution in order to drop its connection to Moffat, leave the mission and establish itself as a nonprofit organization in town.

It appeared, for all intents and purposes, that the custodial relationship codified in the constitution, as discussed in Chapter 4, had come back to haunt the AIG. Instead of mobilizing Moffat's moral authority to vouch for the civic virtue of the AIG and to buffer it against charges of self-seeking financial misconduct, as the original intention of the constitution had been, the gamble of making the AIG an official dependent on the mission looked like it had backfired. If anything, the mission's standing in the constitution as the AIG's fiscal agent and its mandate to appoint the AIG coordinator appeared to give the Williams-Colvin leadership considerable powers over the AIG, putting its standing as an independent organization in jeopardy.

All of this came to a head in May 2005, when Colvin filed charges of insubordination against Kotoloane and suspended him as AIG coordinator. The main charge was the failure on Kotoloane's part to report along established lines of authority and keep his employer, namely Colvin as director of the Kuruman Moffat Mission Trust (KMMT), properly informed. Colvin's memorandum of charges listed eight alleged infractions. Violation of the AIG constitution or attempts to change the constitution figured prominently in Colvin's list, accounting for five of the eight numbered charges that form the grounds of the case against Kotoloane (see Figure 6.2).

As a quasi-legal bureaucratic event, the disciplinary hearing of the charges against Kotoloane by the Moffat board involved two documents – the AIG constitution and Colvin's memorandum of charges. For Colvin, the rhetorical task was to invest the memorandum of charges against Kotoloane with the textual authority of the constitution, to persuade Moffat board members that Kotoloane had indeed violated certain clearly stipulated clauses of the constitution that defined the relationship between the AIG and Moffat. This attempted transfer of textual power across documentary fields, from the constitution to the memorandum of charges, however, failed to take place. Colvin, in effect, was unable to recontextualize the constitution in a way that persuaded the board that insubordination had taken place. The board dismissed the case and apologized to Kotoloane.

You are hereby charged with acts of gross insubordination and bringing the institution of the Kuruman Moffat Mission Trust into disrepute, breach of your duty of good faith towards your employer and/or alternatively being dishonest in the course of your employment.

- Not informing the Director of the KMMT of all meetings of the Executive Committee of the AIG as required in the Constitution.
- Allowing funding proposals to go forward to potential donors without the written consent or knowledge of the Director of the KMMT. (This comes even after a written notice was issued for six months.)
- Having knowledge of and/or assisting in the writing of a proposed new Constitution for the AIG that would remove the AIG from KMMT and placing your signature on the above state document.
- Blatantly assisting and attempting to adopt another Constitution for the AIG without prior knowledge of the Director and attempting to remove AIG from KMMT.
- Not notifying the Director of the KMMT of the abovementioned document.
- Allowing the above document to be presented at an AIG general meeting on 16th March 2005 with the AIG without following proper procedures as outlined in the Constitution.
- Presenting the above document to a staff member of the Asbestos Relief Trust, a donor, for commentary without knowledge of the Director.
- Asserting that your loyalty is not with KMMT.

You will be notified, in a timely manner, should any additional charges be made during the process of the continuing investigation.

Figure 6.2 Larry Colvin, Kuruman Moffat Mission Trust, list of charges against Stephen Kotoloane

Kotoloane's acquittal did not directly refute the lines of authority established in the constitution so much as it ignored them, rendering moot and unenforceable the relationship between the mission and the AIG set forth in the constitution and making it clear by implication that the constitution could not be used to control the AIG. After Kotoloane's acquittal, the AIG constitution was for all practical purposes defunct, not overturned or nullified but rather depleted of the active force it once had. When Colvin sought unsuccessfully to use the constitution as the grounds of Kotoloane's insubordination, the document lost its rhetorical footing and any hold over what people did, freeing the AIG from a constitution that no longer matched the present realities at Moffat. And so the AIG left the mission, registered as a nonprofit organization and opened an office in Kuruman.

The subsequent fate of the AIG was determined by a reconfiguration of forces that replaced the old relation between Moffat and the AIG with new networks linking the AIG to the ART and the municipal government in Kuruman. As the insubordination charges were brewing and the AIG executive committee was actively discussing leaving the mission, Kotoloane consulted with key allies, including Sophia Kisting who was on the ART board of trustees, the ART chair John Doidge and local officials in municipal government, gaining their support in leaving the mission.

In the early years of the post-settlement period, the AIG weathered the organizational crisis with Moffat. Key AIG members moved to new positions. Itumeleng Sithole left MACH and went to work for the ART. Addison Oepeng also left MACH, which was by then in the process of folding, and went to work for the AIG at its new office in town and, along with Kotoloane and Lucia Mokgabl, became the mainstays of AIG office operations until Oepeng retired in 2011. Kotoloane credits Sophia Kisting for her involvement in this redeployment of AIG forces.

The AIG's achievement as a grassroots organization must be measured in part by the role the AIG created for itself on the periphery of mainstream institutions and the standard literacies of elite sectors, where villagers encountered the world of bureaucratic forms and procedures, first in the Gencor case and then in the trust's compensation system. The AIG realized that paperwork was the nexus where the interests of villagers and the ART met and had to be sorted out. In the next section we see what this work looked like on a day-to-day basis, during a morning at the AIG office in Kuruman.

AIG Office Work

It is 1 November 2010, and between 9am and 1pm five people visited or phoned the AIG office. At the time, the AIG was located in the offices of the Duvenhage and van der Mervwe law firm, an approved ART claims handler whose suite also included a small ART office managed by Brenda Sethibeng. Stephen Kotoloane, Addison Oepeng and Lucia Mokgabl were the three paid AIG members who staffed the office. The division of labor in the office was gendered along traditional lines: Kotoloane and Oepeng conferred with visitors; Oepeng consulted the Gefco and Msauli work records that the ART had digitized and worked with contacts at the Chamber of Mines to track down missing work records; and Mokgabl performed clerical tasks. Conversations with visitors took place in Setswana, except for the phone call which Kotoloane conducted in Afrikaans. The AIG office staff spoke to me in English, and Kotoloane and Oepeng translated in summary what had transpired.

Visitor 1: The man from Ncweng

The first visitor was a middle-aged former mineworker from Ncweng who said he had filled out the paperwork to register a claim in the state compensation system and received a letter from the Medical Bureau for Occupational Diseases (MBOD) saying his claim had been approved. He never got any payment, however, and was confused about what to do next. In this case, as Kotoloane explained, the man was encountering the built-in grounds for misunderstanding in the state system that the AIG office had to deal with on a regular basis. This is because the state system has two stages of documentation. First, the mineworker submits to the MBOD the following documents to determine eligibility for compensation:

- Work history
- Clinical examination
- Chest x-ray
- Lung function test
- Information on whether the person has been certified previously
- Histological report on lungs and heart if person is deceased

Based on this information, the MBOD rules on eligibility and notifies the claimant of its decision. In order to be paid, those determined to be eligible for compensation must then submit a second set of documents to the Compensation Commissioner of Occupational Disease (CCOD):

- An application form, with the letter from MBOD
- Verification of work history
- Certified copy of the applicant's ID
- Set of fingerprints
- Salary information (to determine lost wages in calculating amount of compensation)
- Banking details (to deposit the benefit)

It is this two-stage application process, with its two separate sets of documents, that makes for confusion. As a senior MBOD official told the Asbestos Collaborative, once ex-mineworkers receive the letter from MBOD, they often do not realize they must send further documentation to the CCOD and think the compensation money is about to arrive.

As a recurrent situation, Kotoloane's explanation of the two-part process was well-rehearsed, a routine part of AIG office work that clarified the two-stage system and provided the man from Ncweng with an active connection to the paperwork of the state compensation system, which had been stalled.

The case of the man from Ncweng and the state system's two-part process of filing claims is a good example of Kotoloane and Oepeng's expert understanding of a cluster of salient documents and the paper trails involved in filing compensation claims, whether with the trust or with the state. It is important to note that the AIG did not function as claims handlers who prepared the final forms to file. This, as already mentioned, was handled mainly by law firms authorized by the ART. The AIG served rather as an intermediary between villagers and the official submission of documents. The service the AIG invented for itself was that of explaining the paperwork of the metropolis from the point of view of the periphery, mediating the institutional workings of the written record at the local level in order to influence outcomes for villagers at the ART or MBOD.

In this respect, the paperwork of the AIG resembles what has been called 'literacy mediation' (see Baynham & Masing, 2000; Malan, 1996; Robins, 1996) and 'literacy brokering' (see Lillis & Curry, 2006), whereby groups or individuals function socially and linguistically to bridge local and wider contexts. For the AIG, routine office work included assembling and activating a 'genre set' or 'genre system' – a term that denotes how a set of linked documents interact to accomplish a common purpose within a distinct domain of activity.[7] In compensation cases, the genre system consists of mundane documents like work records, ID cards, fingerprints, medical reports, x-rays and lung function tests, application forms and bank details. Each document in the genre system has its own history, institutional presence and field of activity. A medical record that results from an examination in a doctor's office has a very different provenance from a savings account in a bank or the work records of former mineworkers. Each has a high degree of regularity in its textual features, and each functions in predictable ways in the material practices of separate rule-governed bureaucracies. But none presumes or predicts the other. Rather, it was the bureaucratic networks that the MBOD or ART set up to process claims that activated the movement of the documents. The interested activity of AIG office staff supplied the rhetorical motive locally that connected documents and set the genre system into motion for the claimant, thereby producing (or failing to produce) the interaction of the documents desired.

What the AIG came to understand is that there is a *trajectory* to texts, that the forms and records villagers had to manage in making claims are, as Theresa Lillis notes, both *portable*, in that they can be carried by individuals as part of their personal documents or accessed through databases, such as the digitized Gefco and Msauli work records that Oepeng regularly consulted, and *mobile*, in that records and forms can travel to alternative discursive locations, where they intersect with the trajectories of other portable and mobile documents, as in registering a claim (Lillis, 2014: 113–117; also see Maybin, 2017). For the AIG, the paperwork of filing a claim involved recontextualizing documents by moving them from their separate domains of origin and imbuing what would otherwise be disparate and unconnected documents with a joint purpose. This mobilization of texts amplified their potential uses and meaning. The chilling fact is that assembling such a file of documents was meant to establish the certifiability of asbestos-related disease, as monetized by the political economy of compensation created by the Gencor settlement and the state system.

Visitor 2: The young woman from Ga-Mopedi

The second visitor was a young woman from Ga-Mopedi whose father, an ex-mineworker, died in 2004 of mesothelioma, although the family had filed no claim subsequently. She came to the office to see if it was still possible. Kotoloane, who lived in Ga-Mopedi, knew the woman's father and took around an hour to explain what he described later as the 'circumstances and conditions' of the compensation system, in particular the stipulation that the time to file claims with the trust expired three years after a potential claimant's death. This, of course, was disappointing news to the young woman.

The young woman's visit exemplifies a routine side of the AIG's office work that contrasts dramatically with the man from Ncweng. Instead of connecting an ex-mineworker or surviving family member to the compensation system, in the case of the young woman from Ga-Mopedi there was nothing that could be done. The person seeking restitution had already been bypassed by the system, remaining outside the official paperwork where no action is available to pursue with the trust or the state. On the broadest level, this is the predictable outcome of modern compensation systems that use pre-existing statutory standards to determine eligibility and administer benefits under the present socio-economic order in which 'massive demand' is far greater than 'selective access' is designed to provide for. In the case of the ART, as the AIG was well aware, the standards set by the terms of the settlement were applied with every effort to be fair, consistent and honest. Still, as Kotoloane's encounter with the young woman from Ga-Mopedi demonstrates, the terms of eligibility themselves inevitably banish a class of people from access to the paperwork of the system altogether, casting them into a semiotic neverland where their claims cannot enter the official record. The encounter between Kotoloane and the young woman took place in what we might call the negative space of paperwork, a textual vacuum where people are excluded from filling out forms because their time has expired or because of some other technicality. This negative space forms at the margins of paperwork, where motives are vexed and needs remain unsatisfied. Frustration, self-blame, anger and feelings of powerlessness are the byproducts of such encounters with the 'red tape' of official paperwork, as the specific terms of selective access eliminate people from a system whose benefits they would otherwise be entitled to.

Visitor 3: The woman with two small children from Heuningvlei

The third visitor was a woman who had come from Heuningvlei with two small children. Her father worked at the mill in Heunigvlei and had recently died of an undiagnosed respiratory ailment. There was no postmortem histological examination of his cardiorespiratory organs, to which mine and millworkers were entitled by ODMWA statutes. This was a difficult case, Kotoloane knew right away, because the medical evidence necessary to establish a claim was already buried, as had happened so many times in the past. Kotoloane discussed the possibility of going back to the hospital to see if there were any existing medical records the deceased millworker's daughter did not know about that could be used to file a claim.

Kotoloane knew, however, that it was unlikely that anything could be done. As he said after the young mother's visit, 'this one had another body that fell through the cracks,' into the negative space of paperwork. For this reason, the AIG and the ART have carried out awareness campaigns, including public service radio announcements, to demystify organ removal and urge surviving family members to have the postmortems that the MBOD provides deceased mineworkers. Noting the limited availability in rural areas of medical facilities that remove the heart and lungs and then mail the organs to the MBOD to be examined, the AIG and ART have lobbied vigorously for wider access to these services as the necessary gateway to compensation for families of mineworkers who died of undiagnosed respiratory conditions.

Visitor 4: The man from Danielskuil

The fourth visitor was an ex-mineworker from Danielskuil who was seeking information about transportation to the MBOD in Johannesburg for the medical examination to which he was entitled. He was referred to the ART office, where Brenda Sethibeng had been setting up taxis to go to the MBOD. As may be seen, this was a simple case of facilitating access by connecting the man to available resources.

Visitor 5: A phone call from Postmasburg

The fifth person was a woman calling on the phone from Postmasburg, inquiring about 'her claim.' Kotoloane took the call, and Oepeng checked the list of claims filed at the trusts, where her name did not appear. Kotoloane called her back and, after further discussion, realized she was talking about an *insurance* claim, not a claim to the trust or the state compensation system. Having sorted this out, the phone conversation ended, although it left Kotoloane and Oepeng laughing and wondering why the woman had called the AIG in the first place.

The woman's phone call may appear to be no more than a fleeting moment based on a simple misunderstanding that eventually got cleared up. From another angle, however, the episode represents a state of disorientation that is an inevitable part of bureaucratic paperwork. As the AIG office staff well knew, people at times experience an aimless sense of wandering from one office to another, filling out forms or gathering records that seem to accomplish little. In the mazeways of bureaucracy, paperwork can be a distractive medium that misdirects people's attention, leading them to make errant phone calls or send forms to the wrong office or not send them at all. The feeling is like being in a funhouse hall of mirrors, not so much lost as in a perpetual state of bafflement, where you know you are inside a system but no path seems to lead out and every turn hits another dead end.

For the AIG, paperwork consisted not only of documents that were readily stamped and approved, creating 'form-made' persons and moving people's purposes along through the system. As the morning visits to the AIG office show, paperwork was also, as Ben Kafka says, 'uncooperative and unpredictable' (Kafka, 2012: 118), producing disorientation, misapprehension, confusion and the foiling of purposes. The day-to-day paperwork of the AIG cannot be understood without identifying the blockages and textual vacuums that form at the margins of the written record – the negative spaces occupied by villagers who have been bypassed and discarded.

For this reason, moreover, it is not particularly helpful to divide the visits to the AIG office according to how successful they were: whether, that is, the AIG helped someone connect to the compensation system, as in the case of the visitors from Ncweng and Danielskuil, or were unable to do so, as in the case of the women from Ga-Mopedi and Heuningvlei. Such a tally sheet fails to recognize the full extent of what occurred during the office visits and what the AIG brought to bear in the negative spaces where the paperwork collapsed, people's hopes were ruined and their needs went unfulfilled. It is more useful to see how Kotoloane and Oepeng operated as grassroots technicians of paperwork in the political economy of compensation, where they encountered the desires of villagers to become successful 'form-made' claimants and the various obstacles to achieving such a status.

What is distinctive about the AIG, compared to other examples of literacy mediators and literacy brokers, is how their work highlights the periphery of the system, as the location both of the AIG's office work, with its semiotic and geographic distances from metropolitan centers, and of the presence in this work of those who have fallen outside the paperwork of the ART and the state compensation system. As Kotoloane and Oepeng underscored repeatedly in our conversations, the AIG's office work involved not only linking villagers at the periphery to mainstream bureaucratic institutions but also mediating the repercussions of the Gencor settlement and its inevitable disqualifications, when people were turned down by the ART or found they could not even apply. AIG leaders realized that by signing the out-of-court settlement with Gencor on behalf of villagers, they had taken on an obligation to confront the uses and limits of the trust as they played out in the lives of villagers.

In turn, this knowledge of the trust placed a great burden on the AIG office because everyone on the staff understood there would be 'massive demand' but 'selective access.' By 2010, when the episodes above occurred, the AIG had been operating an office in Kuruman for five years and had seen how compensation benefits improved the quality of life for qualifying villagers, how modest purchases of new appliances or furniture made a difference in easing the grinding conditions of poverty. But the AIG office staff also knew with painful certainty that the dashed expectations of villagers were as much an inevitable part of the political economy of compensation as the benefits received by the third who qualified. Any reasonable assessment of the AIG's paperwork must take into account the tempered sorrow that Kotoloane and Oepeng brought to these encounters, as they explained how the system worked, when they knew it bypassed many people and left untold suffering untouched.

In many respects, the year 2010, when the office visits occurred, can be seen as a pivotal moment for the AIG. The volume of claims to the ART had peaked and was in descent – from a high of 425 a month in 2005 to a low of seven in 2013. As a result, the trust decided to restructure its operations, ending the use of claim handlers, turning the filing of claims over to approved medical doctors instead, and closing its local offices in Kuruman, Danielskuil, Burgersfort and Msauli. Following the ART's departure, the AIG coordinated trust-related activity in the Kuruman district, sending potential claimants to trust-accredited medical facilities and helping them retrieve work and other records. As we will see next, in the final section of this chapter, the ART's departure in 2010 also left the AIG at the frontlines, facing a political opposition that had emerged in the post-settlement period to challenge the ART and the AIG.

Rumors and Political Intrigue

Organized opposition to the ART began as early as 2004, with the founding of the Bathlaros-based group Batlaharo Mmogo Reka Dira (BMRD), consisting mainly of ex-National Union of Mineworkers members who believed that all ex-mineworkers who were sick should be paid, not just those who had worked at Gencor mines as the Trust Deed stipulated. The BMRD morphed into the AKC when it was taken over by Cynthia Ndezenka, who moved to the village of Maruping, about 10 miles from Kuruman, where the local AIG affiliate, which was involved in the Gencor case, had recently broken with the AIG leadership. For the incipient forces in Maruping, the case of the ex-mineworker Isaac Matinyane, who died of mesothelioma but was not compensated because he worked at Wandrag – a mine not covered in the Gencor settlement – was a major source of contention with the ART, taken as a sign of the trust's unwillingness to pay those who deserved it.[8]

The first stirrings of the AKC as an oppositional force to the ART and the AIG occurred in late 2008 and early 2009. AKC organized a protest march on the ART office in Kuruman, charging that people with valid claims were not getting paid while others received compensation who should not have. A series of meetings of the AKC, the ART and sometimes Spoor followed over the ensuing years at various levels of government, from the local municipality of Kuruman to the Premier of the Northern Cape, the Deputy Minister of Mineral Resources and ultimately the Master of Court in Pretoria, the state-appointed judicial officer who had oversight of the ART, as is customary in private trusts. During these attempted liaisons, the ART repeatedly asked the AKC to send a list of people who should have received compensation. Such a list was never sent, however, although the AKC continued to make charges about unpaid or improperly paid claims.

Around the time of the AKC protest at the ART office, a delegation of AKC members visited the AIG office, demanding to see the organization's 'documents.' As Kotoloane recalls, the visit felt like a credibility shake-down, a challenge to the AIG's authority waged at the level of documentation and its legitimizing aura in print culture. The AIG showed the AKC visitors its constitution, certificate of incorporation as a nonprofit and the ART Trust Deed. In keeping with its talismanic sense of paperwork, the AKC also asked to see Spoor's 'constitution' which, of course, did not exist. Kotoloane said that the AKC members did not appear to be completely satisfied, but they asked no more questions and left, apparently having exhausted for the moment their inquiry into the AIG's credentials.

It was also around this time in late 2008 and early 2009 that Cynthia Ndezenka was expelled from the AKC. Ndezenka was a legendary con artist who proceeded to take a bag of work records, ID cards and medical files given to her by gullible villagers to appeal for money to a potential benefactor in Cape Town. The iconography of the ex-mineworkers' papers is striking, as sources of authenticity and exchange value, legible and persuasive surrogates of people in need, which Ndezenka transported from the Kuruman district to the philanthropic sector of the metropolis in the suburbs of Cape Town. Ndezenka had a shrewd understanding of the mobility and portability of texts, and the benefactor gave Ndezenka R5000.[9]

In 2010, when the benefactor came to Kuruman to see how the money was being spent, Ndezenka organized a meeting that AIG leaders and municipal officials attended. As Kotoloane reports, Ndenzenka was dressed in an evening gown with a flower in her hair and almost immediately began to attack the mayor of Kuruman for allegedly using the compensation money from the Wandrag mine (which, as just noted, was not covered by either the ART or KRT) to pave the road to Ga-Mopedi. She said that Kotoloane had been fired as the AIG coordinator by the chief at Bathlaros who had asked her to take over the organization. Employing the familiar refrain of the people's vanishing money, she said she saw the trust money in Johannesburg and Pretoria and that she was going to have it transferred to the municipality so villagers could be paid.

The audience, Kotoloane said, were for the most part on Ndezenka's side, caught up by her story of lost money, stolen money, money that exists for the people but has disappeared, money that she will go and get for their benefit. As Addison Oepeng noted, villagers didn't necessarily believe that Spoor had stolen the trust money or that it had disappeared for some mysterious reason, but 'they knew it was possible because the world is a corrupt place.' Oepeng explained that villagers had become suspicious of the trust. The fact that there remained so much money in the trust's account (which, of course, was reserved, according to sound actuarial projections, for future claimants) could easily be taken, he said, as 'a sign the trust was hoarding money and refusing to pay people.' In addition, some villagers 'were starting to say the trust probably was spending it on themselves.' Furthermore, it didn't help, Oepeng said, that Spoor had agreed to keep the terms of the 2006 out-of-court settlement with Eternit that set up the KRT secret, raising questions among villagers about what was being hidden from them.[10]

Rumor played a key role in sustaining these local suspicions about Spoor and the trusts and, by extension, the AIG. Although the rumor that Spoor stole the ART money was demonstrably untrue, the *genre of rumor* operates discursively outside the usual procedures of verification. In their pioneering work, *The Psychology of Rumor*, Gordon Allport and Leo Postman defined rumor as 'a specific (or topical) proposition for belief, passed along from person to person, usually by word of mouth, without secure standards of evidence being present' (quoted in Kapferer, 1990: ix; see Allport & Postman, 1947). Rumor, however, is more than simply a matter of misinformation that can be corrected or, even better, prevented in the first place, as Allport and Postman would have it. Rumor is also the result of the inability of elite sectors to fully control information, to forge an official record based on verifiable standards of evidence that can withstand the onslaught of rumor's misinformation and distorted truths.

To put it another way, the problem of rumor begins not so much with questions of accuracy or inaccuracy but of credibility, of whom you should listen to, whose representation of reality counts, who is entitled to speak. In the ongoing struggle of the professional classes to maintain hegemony in the epistemic registers of knowledge production, rumor becomes a way for ordinary people to withhold or hedge consent to fully delegating authority to the experts. As Jean-Noel Kapferer puts it, what marks rumors is not their 'correctness or incorrectness' but rather their status as an 'unofficial source.' In Kapferer's words, '*A rumor constitutes a relation to authority*: divulging secrets, suggesting hypotheses, it constrains authorities to talk while contesting their status as the sole source authorized to speak' (Kapferer, 1990: 13, 14, italic in original). This, of course, does not mean that rumor is never used in elite sectors, as demagogues like Julius Malema and Donald Trump have made all too clear. It means rather that rumor, in its refusal to abide by the dominant epistemic measures, becomes a readily available rhetorical device for politicians and others to align themselves with the popular classes against the experts.

The point is that the AKC's charges against the ART, precisely because they were rumors, remained unverified and unverifiable, operating in an ideological realm of hypothetical beliefs preserved by the absence of evidence, by the AKC's refusal to compile a list of those wronged by the trust, as the ART requested over and over again. Despite all the meetings between the ART and the AKC, there had been no headway – nor could there be – in agreeing to what constituted the facts at hand or how to establish them. Discussion, in effect, was doomed from the start because the real conflict between the AKC and Spoor, the ART and the AIG was not so much over specific issues as over who was authorized to frame the issues and set the agenda for how the trust's funds should be used.

This stalemate, as already noted, was based in part on an epistemic clash between the professionalized expertise of the ART and the call for popular justice – for *puna kaledi* or 'sorry money' – at the grassroots level. Differing assumptions divided ART officials and villagers. For the ART, the aura of legality invested in the Trust Deed made it axiomatic that compensation was limited to claimants who had worked at or lived near Gencor mines, while it was just as commonsensical to villagers that people's suffering did not differ or have greater or lesser value depending on where they worked or lived. For ART officials, it made perfect sense, according to the available epidemiological studies, that approximately one-third of claimants would be certified to receive compensation by the panel of medical experts at the Lung Institute in Cape Town. To villagers, however, it was just as self-evident that anyone who was listed as a claimant should receive compensation because by giving their name to the litigation they had forced Gencor to create the ART in the first place and to pay for the damage it had done.

These different ways of knowing and understanding, it is important to see, are not a matter of epistemic or cultural relativism but rather require an analysis of social location and the fraught epistemic relations between periphery and center. The underlying conflict between massive demand and selective access reaches across stratified and differentially empowered 'orders of indexicality' that set normative meanings, recognize a hierarchy of discourses and ascribe degrees of epistemic legitimacy. As Blommaert notes, 'systematically reproduced indexicalities are often tied to specific, authoritative actors we call *centring institutions*,' such as the law, medicine, actuarial science, accounting, trust administration, philanthropy and NGOs (Blommaert, 2005: 75, italics in original). The intersection of these domains in the operation of the trust gave the ART its particular socio-epistemic identity as a mainstream institution based on professional expertise.

On the other hand, while it is true that in metropolitan settings such centring institutions typically exert a centripetal pull, generating 'indexicalities to which others have to orient in order to be "social," i.e. to produce meanings that "belong" somewhere,' this differs at the grassroots level, where local orders of indexicality can exert a destabilizing centrifugal force that creates friction with the hegemonic order. The collision of incommensurable meaning-making systems produced a stand-off between the grassroots notion of 'sorry money' and the trust's medico-legal monetization of asbestos-related disease. This was, in effect, a showdown between the forces of popular justice in the villages (as motivated by the recurring question of '*how to get out of our present troubles*') and the official consciousness of the trust (as motivated by the question of its reputation for fair and efficient administration of the Trust Deed). These were the discursive grounds – the epistemic registers – that divided grassroots and metropolitan spheres of influence in the aftermath of the Gencor settlement.

Interwoven, certainly, were material interests. On the part of the ART's professional managerial regime, the interest in establishing and preserving the epistemic authority of the trust was entangled with the ART's institutional need to justify how it spent the settlement money. As we have seen, the ART's credit worthiness (in terms of both its semiotic and economic value) relied on specialized monopolies of expertise and mainstream institutions of professional practice. On the other hand, in Maruping, the AKC had a material interest in prolonging the lack of resolution with the ART in order to maintain a sense of grievance among its membership and invest the organization with an urgent sense of mission.

According to Kotoloane and Oepeng, the AKC's main goal was not to solve problems or negotiate differences but simply to continue as an organization. Unlike the village-based AIG, Kotoloane and Oepeng emphasized, the AKC, which was registered as a nonprofit, was based on individual memberships. The AKC charged R450 to register as a member. In turn, members were charged R2 for each weekly meeting, with occasional levies for special purposes such as the AKC leadership's travel to meetings in Kimberley or Pretoria.

The goal of preserving the involvement of its membership and the flow of fees created a logic of escalation, as was evident when the AKC disrupted an AIG meeting in Ga-Mopedi in 2013. As Kotoloane recounts, an AKC member interrupted the meeting just after it had started, demanding to know who had given the AIG the right to hold such a meeting (which in this case was the chief at Ga-Mopedi, who had invited the AIG) and who the AIG was working for. Kotoloane ignored the questions and gave his standard presentation, at the end of which an AKC member stood up to say:

> I'll fight till the death for people's rights, for people's money. It's being eaten. It's been happening for a long time. Now is enough. If you could see, Stephen has a big car and a big house. With your money. Come to Maruping, meeting every Wednesday. The case is now with the Master of Court.

After the meeting, an AKC member told Kotoloane, 'We came to Kuruman. If you had been in your office, we would have killed you. This must be the last meeting.' The next day, Kotoloane filed charges of threat and intimidation with the local police. In response, AKC's lawyer sent Kotoloane a letter demanding R2 million for defamation.[11]

By this point in 2013, the AKC's attacks on the ART had found a legal outlet, after Sylvia Lucas, the Premier of the Northern Cape, agreed to take the AKC's charges against the ART to the Master of Court in Pretoria. Maruping was a longtime ANC stronghold, and AKC leaders used their political connections in Kimberley to make the usual case of 'maladministration' on the ART's part, arguing that some people who were qualified did not get compensation and some who did were not qualified. In addition, in a special bid to its membership, the AKC demanded from the trust an *ex gratia* payment of R30 million, to be paid to AKC members who were claimants in the Gencor case, whether or not they had contracted an asbestos-related disease, for lending their names to the litigation.

The case was eventually thrown out in 2015 by the North Gauteng High Court, which ruled that the AKC failed to establish *locus standi* in court – that it never made a legal argument for its charges against the ART or produced the list of villagers who should have received compensation or the affidavits it had promised to establish the community's interest in the operations of the ART. The judge said further that it was 'unreasonable' in the first place for the Premier's office to have filed the AKC's complaint with the Master of Court and that the AKC's demand to pay people who do not qualify in terms of the ART Trust Deed was 'irrational.'

The ruling was a devastating dismissal of the AKC's flimsy rumor-dependent legal strategy, but it did not deter the AKC, which has continued to spread rumors and make unfounded accusations against the trusts and the AIG. As recently as 2018, Thabang Selo, an AKC organizer, was quoted in a *Mail & Guardian* news report as saying that there is 'R400-million sitting in an account somewhere' and not getting through to the people. 'We have gone to every office. We have marched to the Union Buildings. No one wants to help us. No one wants to tell us what happened to our money. Maybe now Ramaphosa can help us,' Selo said (Ledwaba, 2018).

The AIG in a World of Rumors and Intrigue

Throughout the unsettled years following the Gencor settlement, the AIG was sustained by its understanding that villagers in the opposition were suffering and in desperate need. To be sure, as a strictly not-for-profit village-based organization, the AIG worried about low-level corruption in the AKC and the fees and levies it charged its members. The AIG knew how the infusion of cash by the ART had created a political economy of compensation that seeped at its edges into the villages, creating opportunities for grassroots hustles, from the petty criminality of sharks who defrauded ex-mineworkers to the civil society sector and groups like the AKC with political connections, riding on rumor, innuendo and promises that could never be fulfilled but that spoke to real needs.

The AIG's familiarity with the details of the Gencor settlement produced an intimate awareness of how the ART's compensation system played out unevenly in the lives of villagers, giving the activists a special knowledge of what the trust enabled those who qualified for benefits to do and who it bypassed and left untouched. The AIG's stance was to vouch for the integrity of the ART – that the trust was honest and followed the rules it had made – but without justifying the terms of eligibility for compensation set by the Trust Deed. The AIG viewed itself as prior to the ART, as the grassroots network of villages that helped bring the ART into existence. As Stephen Kotoloane put it, the AIG was an ally but not a 'shield for the trust.'[12]

In a world of rumors and political intrigue, the AIG held that villagers were entitled to believe whatever they liked, but that if they wanted accurate information about the trust or the state compensation system they should come to the AIG office. The AIG's stance was meant to be informative – to promote popular understanding of the workings of the trusts and the MBOD – but not neutral in its alignment with villagers' interests and needs. This was enough during the turbulent years to preserve the AIG's standing as honest representatives of the community who had given their word to explain the uses and limits of the Gencor and Eternit settlements.

If anything, the rumors spread by Cynthia Ndezenka and the AKC may have helped, in a curious way, to keep villagers' attention focused on the ART and to mobilize people to visit the AIG office. Visits to the office in Kuruman never declined, and the work the AIG did in the schools, in monitoring rehabilitation sites and in visiting the sick continued at the usual pace.

Notes

(1) In important respects, the Gencor settlement went beyond the state compensation system. Most prominent was the landmark achievement of including environmental as well as occupational exposures as the grounds for compensation. There were also other distinctive features in the settlement, for example: the compensation for 'mild' lung function impairment (whereas the state system was limited to 'moderate' and 'severe'); the mandate to actively solicit claims from potentially eligible ex-mineworkers or families of deceased mineworkers (whereas the state system had no outreach operations); the emphasis on efficiency in processing claims (whereas the time had reached four years or more in the state system); and the decision to pay the fees for medical examinations (the state provided exams every two years) and claims handling (whereas the state did not cover this cost). Unlike the state compensation system, the ART was pro-active in a variety of ways, including: the training of

doctors and other health care providers to use spirometers, read x-rays and diagnose asbestos-related disease; the funding of a palliative care nurse in Kuruman; lobbying on behalf of ban-asbestos legislation in South Africa; and support for the anti-asbestos movement worldwide.

(2) Trustees were chosen by various stakeholders: two by Ntuli, Noble and Spoor on behalf of the litigants; one by Gencor; one by Gefco/Msauli; and the fifth agreed on by all parties. Important to the AIG, as we will see in a moment, Sophie Kisting was one of the original trustees; later Phiroshaw Camay, activist and struggle veteran, became a KRT trustee.

(3) The management of the ART itself was initially outsourced for a period of time to the Maitland Trust, a privately owned firm specializing in fund administration and other fiduciary services. Taquanta Asset Managers, a division of Nedbank, handled the trust's investment portfolio. Lucro Auditing (and earlier KPMG) performed the annual audits of the ART's financial activity. In 2008 the ART bought a unit in a Johannesburg office building to serve as headquarters, and now rents space, as trust operations have been winding down.

(4) This included benefits for Herman Kubari, the lead plaintiff on the founding affidavit in the Gencor case, who was dying of mesothelioma when the settlement was made.

(5) On GEAR, see, for example, Bond (2000), Alexander (2002) and Marais (2011).

(6) Kotoloane claimed that the Moffat leadership of Williams and Colvin used up to R50,000 of AIG funds for other mission purposes. Interview by author, 1 November 2010.

(7) On the terms 'genre sets' and 'genre systems,' see Devitt (2004).

(8) Tina Da Cruz, interview by author, 16 June 2011.

(9) Stephen Kotoloane, interview by author, 1 November 2010. See also Koikanyang (2010: 2).

(10) Addison Oepeng, interview by author, 21 June 2011.

(11) Stephen Kotoloane, interview by author, 7 August 2013.

(12) Stephen Kotoloane, interview by author, 20 June 2011.

Conclusion: Grassroots Activism, Popular Participation and Contextual Spaces

Figure C.1 Photograph by David Goldblatt
Blue asbestos waste on the Owendale Asbestos Mine tailings dump, Near Postmasburg, Northern Cape. 21 December 2002

Figure C.2 Photograph by David Goldblatt
Tailings dump after reclamation, Owendale Asbestos Mine, Northern Cape. 24 December 2007

As we saw in the last chapter, the AIG's day-to-day encounters with the paperwork of filing claims with the ART made the office staff in Kuruman acutely aware of the uses and limits of the trust's compensation system. AIG activists witnessed how benefits enhanced the lives of those who qualified and how disqualification played out in the disappointment and frustration of those who did not. At the same time, the AIG also realized that the monetization of disease itself – in the form of scheduled payouts to individual claimants – posed a certain dilemma, namely that compensation always happens after the fact, when it can mitigate pain and suffering but not remove the conditions that led to the pain and suffering in the first place. For the AIG, the payment of individual claims was fully justified by the harm caused by the asbestos industry. The problem was that the payment of damages for personal injury could not prevent the exposure of present and future generations to deadly asbestos fibers or build medical clinics and research facilities to treat asbestos-related disease.

For these reasons, the AIG looked in two directions. On the one hand, the AIG pushed for expanding eligibility for compensation under the ART by: (1) extending the expiration date for filing a claim from three to at least five or, even better, seven years (whereby the woman from Ga-Mopedi in the previous chapter would not have been excluded); (2) increasing the number of claims based on environmental exposures, a historic but underutilized feature of the Trust Deed which accounted for less than 1% of claims filed (Ndlovu *et al.*, 2013: 84); and (3) lifting the restriction that only spouses and children under 18 of deceased mineworkers were eligible to file a claim. This limitation, the AIG argued, was based on the middle-class nuclear family and failed to take into account how extended families among the black rural working class often depended on mineworkers' wages. The AIG also argued that differences in individual benefits based on job category and projected loss of income should be eliminated because they reproduced the racialized division of labor and wage scales on the mines. As Kotoloane put it, 'the pain and suffering of asbestos-related disease victims are the same' and should be compensated accordingly.

On the other hand, even before the Gencor case ended in 2003, AIG members and allies from elite sectors were raising questions beyond individual compensation about restitution for historic wrongs and social reparations for the protection of life. There was talk, for example, among AIG activists in Kuruman about devoting 3% or 4% of the Gencor settlement money to rehabilitating secondary environmental contamination. Likewise, on the medical front, 'In those early days,' Sophia Kisting writes, 'we dreamt about the possibility of establishing a "Centre of Excellence" in Kuruman to diagnose and effectively manage and provide on-going training on the many asbestos-related health problems encountered' (Asbestos Relief Trust, n.d.). A few years later, Stephen Kotoloane and Richard Aitken raised similar hopes about using funds from the impending 2006 settlement with Eternit to set up a medical and research center in Kuruman. Finally, in a memorandum to the premier of the Northern Cape, presented at a 2010 demonstration in Kimberley, the AIG called for a Superfund/Asbestos Development Fund, with significant state funding to augment the trusts, for rehabilitation, increased compensation and expanded medical services.

The principle of justice at work in the AIG's proposals was restitution: to redistribute the gains of ill-gotten wealth in order to repair the damage done by the asbestos industry and the state and to ensure healthy living conditions for all who reside in the former mining districts. In this regard, the AIG's notion of restitution as amends for historic wrongs resembled the popular understanding of *puna kaledi* or 'sorry money.' A key difference, however, was that the AIG's vision of *social* reparations included individual compensation but also imagined redistributing forms of cultural capital, such as technical expertise, agenda-setting powers and access to forums of deliberation and decision making about the compensation system, the rehabilitation of the environment and the provision of medical care. Building on the participatory shop floor research projects of the Industrial Health Research Group (IHRG) and the 1998 National Asbestos Summit's unrealized call for union and community involvement, the AIG wanted villagers to be recognized not just as victims of the asbestos catastrophe but as sources of grassroots knowledge and active participants in addressing the disastrous legacy of the asbestos industry.

One of the central questions to emerge in this book from the entangled histories of grassroots activism, insurgent lawfare and workers' compensation systems is how popular participation by villagers living on the margins of the world system was enabled and constrained by the relations of elite and grassroots sectors, experts and lay people, official and popular consciousness, metropolitan and peripheral spheres of influence. In the final pages of this book, I want to step back for a moment to consider more directly the various articulations of popular participation that have already appeared in earlier chapters.

There are two main reasons to do so. The first, as was just suggested, is that the question of participation is inherent to the main themes of the book: participation is what connects or fails to connect grassroots literacy to the written record; it is a measure of rhetorical agency and epistemic power; it determines whose questions count in the production of knowledge and public policy.

The second reason is related to – and helps explain – the first by posing the question of participation more broadly as one of social justice. As Nancy Fraser puts it, 'the most general meaning of justice is parity of participation':

> According to this radical-democratic interpretation of equal moral worth, justice requires social arrangements that permit all to participate as peers in social life. Overcoming injustice means dismantling institutionalized obstacles that prevent some people from participating on a par with others, as full partners in social interaction. (Fraser, 2005: 73)

The obstacles to participation that Fraser details are familiar features of life and literacy in the Kuruman district: 'people can be impeded from full participation,' she says, 'by economic structures that deny them the resources they need to interact with others as peers,' as well as by 'institutionalized hierarchies of cultural value that deny them the requisite standing' (Fraser, 2005: 73; see also Fraser, 1990: 56–80).

In Fraser's view, theories of justice must include not only the economic dimension of *distribution* (the 'what') and the cultural dimension of *recognition* (the 'who'), but also the political dimension of *representation* – the question of 'how' people participate in a shared social world. What is especially useful about Fraser's notion of 'participatory parity' is that it provides a normative measure to make sense of many of the key concepts in this book – the asymmetrical access to epistemic agency, the semiotic distance between periphery and center, the stratified orders of indexicality. In Fraser's three-dimensional conception of justice, the question of distribution/redistribution (of semiotic resources, compensation money, medical services, and so on) and recognition (of legal standing, rhetorical footing, epistemic authority, and so on) hinges on the participation (or its absence) of ordinary people in a deliberative democracy. For Fraser, the 'deep internal connections between democracy and justice' point to the need for participatory institutional arenas in which the vast majority of people, now excluded by elite monopolies of power and influence, can 'engage on terms of parity in decision-making' (Fraser, 2005: 85).

As a textual history of the AIG, this book has been concerned to a large extent with what Blommaert calls '*differential access to forms*, to linguistic/communicative resources, resulting in differential capacities to accomplish certain functions' (Blommaert, 2005: 76, italics in original). For an example, recall how, in Chapter 1, the AIG's 'differential access' to a standard form of mainstream literacy, i.e. the monthly report, provided the pretext for an ART official to refuse to map the AIG's partial realization of form onto function, such as keeping a paper trail, accounting to donors, projecting an organizational presence, and so on. But if differential access to meaning-making resources haunts the relation of periphery and center, Blommaert adds a second key consideration when he notes that the question of 'differential access to contextual spaces, i.e. spaces of meaning ratification where specific forms conventionally receive specific functions' is equally important in understanding how semiotic inequality works in the world, 'resulting ... in differential capacity to *interpret*' (Blommaert, 2005: 76, italics in original).

What Blommaert helps us see is that differential access to the 'contextual spaces' of knowledge production and policy making, as well as access to forms, shapes the available possibilities of popular participation in any given situation. Such contextual spaces, as Richard Bauman and Charles L. Briggs have argued, are not 'discourse external' containers that surround communicative acts but arise instead from processes of contextualization that people draw upon to interpret situations, utterances, texts, and so forth (Bauman & Briggs, 1990). In this sense, context is always performative, always emergent, co-constructed dialogically by relevant participants and hence a matter of practice. But contextual spaces are also the observable results of such practices of contextualization sedimented over time, giving what John Gumperz calls 'systems of contextualizaton conventions' the appearance of continuity, solidity and stability (Gumperz, 1992). This is what makes the institutional frameworks and forums that concern us here seem to come equipped in advance with densely settled histories, patterns of operation and means of reproduction that can enable, but all too frequently constrain, relations of participatory parity and the capacity of ordinary people to interpret the world in ways that have consequence.

At the risk of being overly schematic, we might identify three different modalities of popular participation – three different linkages between grassroots and elite sectors – that have appeared in earlier chapters. As we will see, each presents a different configuration of knowledge production and policy making, shaped by differing relationships between popular participation and contextual spaces:

(1) The service function model: ART and AIG

As emphasized at many points in the previous chapter, the terms of the Gencor settlement were set by professionals in well-demarcated metropolitan domains (medical, actuarial, legal, scientific, and so on). The ART's reliance on experts from the professional managerial classes left the AIG's grassroots understandings suspended at the margins of the trust. It is not that ART officials failed to hear – or even to be sympathetic toward – AIG input, such as its proposals to expand eligibility, just listed above. The problem was that the AIG's popular knowledge was separated by its unequal epistemic standing, and no institutional frameworks or forums – no contextual spaces – existed that enabled grassroots activists to participate in and influence the specialized deliberations that made trust policy. The AIG, for example, never held a seat on the ART or KRT's board of trustees. For the most part, the AIG was seen as a service organization and community liaison, good at transmitting accurate information from the trust about the trust but not knowledge generating or policy making in its own capacity.

One problem with this characterization of the AIG as a service organization is that it fails to recognize the extent to which the AIG's routine office work, as well as its proposals to expand or change the terms of eligibility for compensation, grew out of the close reading, textual analysis and interpretation of a host of documents (the Trust Deed, ART policies, ODMWA statutes, MBOD procedures, and so on). This close reading was the necessary foundation of the AIG's work on filing claims, giving AIG activists an intimate familiarity with the paperwork and operating policies of the ART and the state compensation system. The point, however, is that the close reading required of AIG activists cannot be explained simply as the service function of a 'community partner.' It was also a popular form of critical practice, a variant of the 'normal' intellectual work with texts in academia, the professions, the world of letters and other mainstream spaces, actualized on the periphery by organic intellectuals at the grassroots level.

Consider, for example, how the linked processes of decontextualization and recontextualization appear as discursive strategies of inquiry and interpretation in the AIG's proposals to eliminate compensation based on formerly racialized wage scales and expand eligibility for compensation to relatives beyond the nuclear family. The AIG began by decontextualizing ART documents that set the terms of compensation, detaching them from their original contexts of production and use in the trusts, altering their trajectories and moving them, across social locations, to a new contextual space. In effect, the ART documents were (re)localized, their textual potentialities for meaning making reset in a 'locus of enunciation' that subjected them to the geohistorical gaze of the periphery. To put it another way, the AIG's grassroots scrutiny recontextualized ART documents by reframing them 'from below,' bringing to light the ethnocentric assumptions and residues of racial hierarchy that had been naturalized in trust policy and thereby rendered unavailable for analysis. In this sense, the decontextualization of ART documents *made them available* to be recoded as inadequate to the realities and needs of villagers living in the former asbestos mining districts. In turn, the AIG's recontextualization amounted to the rewriting of metropolitan documents in the epistemic register of grassroots activists to realign the discourse of compensation to the interests of villagers.

As Antonio Gramsci put it in his classic analysis of traditional and organic intellectuals in the *Prison Notebooks*, 'All men [sic] are intellectuals, one could therefore say: but not all men [sic] have in society the function of intellectuals' (Gramsci, 1971: 140). In the ART's networks of expertise, there was no contextual space for the AIG to occupy in the 'function of intellectuals.' Popular participation was derailed, limited to the imaginary realm of 'community work,' as the ART's epistemic regime bypassed the AIG. The intellectual work of the AIG's close reading, textual analysis and interpretation/reinterpretation remained unrecognized and unratified, outside the ART's institutional frameworks and forums.

(2) Partial participation and the delegation of rhetorical agency: Lawyer and client relations

In Chapter 5, we looked at the dynamics of agency and submission in the creation of 'form-made' persons, such as the clients and claimants of insurgent lawfare in the Gencor case. As we saw, mass mobilizations at the grassroots level combined with Richard Spoor's revisionist legal arguments to lift the veil of employer immunity in the no-fault state compensation system and thereby to enable ex-mineworkers and surviving family members to gain voice and participate in previously inaccessible legal forums under the common law. This merger of activity across grassroots and elite sectors was a large part of what made the lawfare insurgent.

Still, given the asymmetry of the expert/lay relations of lawyer and client, popular participation in the Gencor case was partial and truncated. As litigants gained legal and rhetorical standing to testify before the court, their participation was qualified by the 'power of substitution' clause that delegated to lawyers the authority to speak and act with 'unfettered discretion' on their clients' behalf. Such a delegation of authority, as we saw Marie-Andrée Jacob argue, can indeed enable individuals and groups to achieve particular goals through the institutionally channeled agency of 'putting yourself in the hands of experts.' At the same time, these institutional frameworks of professional practice are meant to perform gate-keeping functions – to exclude parity of participation by the uncredentialed in order to preserve the exchange value of professional work through monopolies of expertise. Spoor's entextualization of his clients' verbal testimony as legal evidence in the founding affidavit of the Gencor case is emblematic not just of the textual dynamics of lawyer/client relations but more generally of how monopolies of accredited expertise and their institutional frameworks – in medicine, public health, social work, education, and so on – distribute rhetorical agency across the unequal relations between professionals and laypeople in the administered societies of late capitalism.

This does not mean, of course, that alliances across grassroots and elite sectors – between community groups and professionals from a broad range of fields – should be avoided. It means rather that the relationships with professionals that grassroots organizations must often depend on to gain access to the legal system, medical services, government agencies and other mainstream institutions are fraught with structural and semiotic inequalities that undermine parity of participation. This is in part what produced popular suspicions and class resentments in the aftermath of the Gencor case, giving rise to rumors like 'the lawyer stole the money' and making the forums set up to mediate differences between the trust and Asbestos Kgatelopele Community so hopelessly ineffectual. It is also why, as we have seen, the AIG developed a dual approach to the Gencor case and its aftermath, participating from the *inside* as community legal workers, plaintiffs on the founding affidavit, a signatory to the out-of-court settlement and a source of popular understanding of the trusts' compensation system, and from the *outside* as the community watchdog, monitoring the effects of the case and its settlement as they played out in the lives of villagers.

(3) Participatory research projects: Intertwining popular and elite knowledges

We saw in Chapter 3 the epistemic valuing of shop floor experience and the intertwining of worker-generated and expert knowledge in the Industrial Health Research Group's (IHRG) research projects. In Chapter 4, we saw how the IHRG's participatory modes of knowledge production, along with the Asbestos Collaborative's grassroots-oriented Participatory Rural Appraisal (PRA) workshops, offered models for the AIG's village-based research, such as the household surveys and the mapping of asbestos contamination. We saw further how AIG maps entered into the research design and AIG activists participated as fieldworkers in Robert R. Jones' state-funded research on secondary asbestos contamination for Conservation Support Services (CSS).

These three participatory research projects offer variations on the common theme of realigning professional expertise to grassroots knowledges, revealing different institutional frameworks and forums of popular participation and different styles of addressing the issue of *whose* questions are being raised:

- The PRA workshops that Fano Endor ran for the Asbestos Collaborative in 2001 provided a well-established Freirean methodology for villagers to identify the sources of their troubles and to plan actions accordingly. The professional input was that of a facilitator in solidarity with local communities, to raise consciousness (*conscientização*) at the grassroots level through a 'pedagogy of the oppressed.'
- The IHRG's union-based participatory research projects, on the other hand, were more explicitly joint activities in which the focus of research (*whose* questions) emerged as the result of agenda-setting dialogues across social divisions between elite and grassroots sectors. The goal was not simply to activate worker-generated knowledge at the grassroots level but to intertwine shop floor understandings with the professional knowledges of radicalized occupational health activists.
- The CSS research project offers a brief glimpse into what popular participation in government-sponsored research on secondary asbestos pollution might look like in practice, as the basis of large-scale public works projects to remove or contain the sources of asbestos contamination in the built environment, derelict dumps, the tailings used in roads, and so on. As we saw, this was one of the main goals of the 1998 National Asbestos Summit taken up by occupational health activists like Sophia Kisting, as well as by villagers from Ncweng and elsewhere. If the vision remains unrealized, its moving parts are nonetheless relevant as an anticipation of what could be: popular participation at the grassroots level (as field researchers, policy planners, abatement workers, and so on); the meshing of elite and grassroots knowledges (such as the CSS's integration of AIG maps into its research design); and the allocation by the South African state of major resources to research secondary asbestos pollution, to redistribute technical expertise in rehabilitation (in a skills transfer from Eko Rehab's monopolistic grip) and to ensure healthy conditions of life (the biological citizenship guaranteed to all South Africans by the post-apartheid constitution).

It is important not to delude ourselves about the prospects of participatory parity in contemporary class society, where the necessary resources and contextual spaces of knowledge production and policymaking are so unequally distributed or non-existent. Parity of participation figures here in our reading of the CSS project (and more generally) as a critical horizon, an indispensable if counterfactual normative condition that enables us: (1) to see the limits of 'open access' to participation in the formally inclusive institutional frameworks and forums of late capitalism (i.e. voting, corporate multiculturalism, compulsory public education, equal economic opportunity programs, and so on); and (2) to imagine the capacity of alternative and subaltern 'contextual spaces' to engender new social solidarities and new social futures.

Nancy Fraser's formative work on subaltern public spheres has been especially useful in drawing attention to the 'discursive arenas where members of subordinated social groups invent and circulate counterdiscourses, which in turn permit them to formulate oppositional interpretations of their identities, interests, and needs' (Fraser, 1990: 67). As she suggests, it is not the contextual spaces themselves but the social interactions they enable that produce and disseminate 'counterdiscourses' and 'oppositional interpretations.' In the realm of asbestos activism, such 'discursive arenas' have reached across grassroots and elite sectors to intertwine shop floor and village-based grassroots knowledges with radicalized professional expertise. Asymmetrical divisions of labor and the semiotic gaps they produce cannot simply be dissolved or wished away in the present social order but, as participatory research projects have shown, they can be recalibrated and realigned, away from the monopolistic hold of gate-keeping institutions at the center to contextual spaces at the margins that foster relations of solidarity, joint agenda-setting and parity of participation *with differences*.

The upshot, it seems to me, is that grassroots organizations like the AIG are not so much in need of *more* knowledge and information, as though they were empty and had to be filled up by well-meaning benefactors from the NGO world of capacity building, skills transfer and human capital development. Instead, the need at the grassroots is to change the modalities of participation in knowledge production in order to change the nature of the knowledge produced. The shift, as we have seen, is toward a vision of *socially useful knowledge* – knowledge that referred, in the annals of working-class radicalism, to learning that was devoted to neither capitalist utility nor bourgeois cultivation of self but rather to the urgent question of '*how to get out of our present troubles*' (see Johnson, 1979).

*****

The last time I saw Stephen Kotoloane was over several days in August 2013, not long after members of the Asbestos Kgatelopele Community had disrupted the AIG meeting in Ga-Mopedi. The threat of violence had shaken Kotoloane, seeming all the more ominous against the backdrop of heightened political violence at that time in South Africa. But he had not been rattled at the core. Kotoloane knew why the disruption had happened and how popular discontent grows out of desperate living conditions. He also knew that the era of compensation and its fraught entanglements were passing and the ART was winding down. Our conversation turned to the AIG's next step, away from the dilemmas of the payout-for-personal-injury model of compensation to a new focus on secondary asbestos contamination in school buildings and the prospects of building a coalition of the AIG, parents, students, teachers and their union to lobby for rehabilitation and safe schools.

Stephen Kotoloane died two years later in 2015. He never saw the coalition fully develop, and his legacy was turned over to his daughter Prudence who now directs the AIG. What has stayed with me, though, from that last visit, was Stephen's abiding equanimity in the face of the AKC and his foresight, looking ahead with a renewed sense of urgency, to the creation of a new coalition – to continue the work the AIG started over a decade ago through new alliances across grassroots and elite sectors and new contextual spaces on the periphery for popular participation.

References

Abdullah, M.F. and Manjra, S.J. (1992) *The Kuruman Asbestos Report.* Cape Town: Industrial Health Research Group, University of Cape Town.

Action Youth (1984) Black Allied Mining and Construction Workers Union. *Arise Vukani* 1 (1), 5–6. See https://disa.ukzn.ac.za/AvSep8416848098001001Sep19849 (accessed March 2020).

Alexander, N. (2002) *An Ordinary Country: Issues in the Transition from Apartheid to Democracy in South Africa.* Scottsville: University of Natal Press.

Allen, L.K. (2011) Ban asbestos phenomenon: The winds of change. *New Solutions* 21 (4), 629–636.

Allen, V.L. (2005) *Organise or Die, 1982–1994: The History of Black Mineworkers in South Africa.* Keighley: Moor Press.

Allport, G. and Postman, L. (1947) *The Psychology of Rumor.* New York: Henry Holt.

Ally, N. and Ally, S. (2008) Critical intellectualism: The role of black consciousness in reconfiguring the race–class problematic in South Africa. In A. Mngxitama, A. Alexander and N. Gibson (eds) *Biko Lives! Contesting the Legacies of Steve Biko* (pp. 171–188). New York: Palgrave Macmillan.

Amin, S. (1974) *Accumulation on a World Scale: A Critique of the Theory of Underdevelopment.* New York: Monthly Review Press.

Anderson, B. (1991) *Imagined Communities: Reflections on the Origin and Spread of Nationalism.* London: Verso.

Aron, J. and Myers, J. (1989) Asbestos and asbestos-related disease in South Africa: An update. SALDRU Working Paper No. 71. Cape Town: Southern Africa Labour and Development Research Unit.

AC (Asbestos Collaborative) (2001) *Asbestos-related Disease in South Africa: Opportunities and Challenges Remaining Since the 1998 Parliamentary Asbestos Summit.* Report to the Parliamentary Portfolio Committee on Environmental Affairs and Tourism, 12 October.

Asbestos Relief Trust (n.d.) A Ten-year History, 2003–2013. Unpublished pdf.

Balshem, M. (1993) *Cancer in the Community: Class and Medical Authority.* Washington, DC: Smithsonian Books.

BAMCU (Black Allied Mining & Construction Workers' Union) (1984) Asbestos: A Position Paper by BAMCU, 11 October.

Barber, K. (ed.) (2006) *Africa's Hidden Histories: Everyday Literacy and Making the Self.* Bloomington, IN: Indiana University Press.

Bauman, R. and Briggs, C.L. (1990) Poetics and performance as critical perspectives on language and social life. *Annual Review of Anthropology* 19, 59–88.

Baynham, M. and Masing, H.L. (2000) Mediators and mediation in multilingual literacy events. In M. Martin-Jones and K. Jones (eds) *Multilingual Literacies: Reading and Writing in Different Worlds* (pp. 189–207). Amsterdam: John Benjamins.

Bazerman, C. (1988) *Shaping Written Knowledge: The Genre and Activity of the Experimental Article in Science.* Madison, WI: University of Wisconsin Press.

Bell, D. (1973) *The Coming of Post-industrial Society.* New York: Basic Books.

BizNews (2014) Poor diagnosis deprives SA miners of compensation. *Biz News*, 22 October. See https://www.biznews.com/africa/2014/10/22/poor-diagnosis-deprives-sa-asbestos-miners-compensation.

Blommaert, J. (2005) *Discourse*. Cambridge: Cambridge University Press.

Blommaert, J. (2008) *Grassroots Literacy: Writing, Identity, and Voice in Central Africa*. London: Routledge.

Blommaert, J. (2010) *The Sociolinguistics of Globalization*. Cambridge: Cambridge University Press.

Blommaert, J. (2013) *Ethnography, Superdiversity and Linguistic Landscapes: Chronicles of Complexity*. Bristol: Multilingual Matters.

Blommaert, J., Muyllaert, N., Huysmans, M. and Dyers, C. (2005) Peripheral normativity: Literacy and the production of locality in a South African township. *Linguistics and Education* 16 (3), 378–403.

Bond, P. (2000) *Elite Transition: From Apartheid to Neoliberalism in South Africa*. London: Pluto Press.

Braun, L. (2014) *Breathing Race into the Machine: The Surprising Career of the Spirometer from Plantation to Genetics*. Minneapolis, MN: University of Minnesota Press.

Braun, L. and Kisting, S. (2006) Asbestos-related disease in South Africa: The social production of an invisible epidemic. *Journal of American Public Health* 99 (8), 1386–1396.

Braun, L. and Kopinski, H. (2018) Causal understandings: Controversy, social context, and mesothelioma. *BioSocieties* 13 (3), 557–579.

Breckenridge, K. (2012) No will to know: The rise and fall of civil registration in twentieth-century South Africa. In K. Breckenridge and S. Szreter (eds) *Registration and Recognition: Documenting the Person in World History* (pp. 357–383). Oxford: Oxford University Press.

Brodeur, D. (1985) *Outrageous Misconduct; The Asbestos Industry on Trial*. New York: Pantheon Books.

Brown, P. (1987) Popular epidemiology: Community response to toxic waste-induced disease in Woburn, Massachusetts. *Science, Technology & Human Values* 12 (3 & 4).

Bulembu (2017) Press release: Kobolondo Mining and Bulembu Ministries Swaziland sign option agreement. *Bulembu*, 29 June.

Bundy, C. (1979) *The Rise and Fall of the South African Peasantry*. Berkeley, CA: University of California Press.

Butler, J. and Athanasiou, A. (2013) *Dispossession: The Performative in the Political*. Cambridge: Polity Press.

Canagarajah, S. (2002) *A Geopolitics of Academic Writing*. Pittsburgh, PA: University of Pittsburgh Press.

Cape Asbestos South Africa (1968) *Progress at Penge*. Johannesburg: Cape Asbestos South Africa (Pty) Ltd.

Chambers, R. (1994) The origins and practice of participatory rural appraisal. *World Development* 22 (7), 953–969.

Clanchy, M. (1979) *From Memory to Written Record: England 1066–1307*. Cambridge, MA: Harvard University Press.

Comaroff, J.L. (2001) Colonialism, culture, and the law: A foreword. *Law & Social Inquiry* 26 (2), 305–314.

Comaroff, J.L. and Comaroff, J. (2006) Law and disorder in the postcolony. In J. Comaroff and J.L. Comaroff (eds) *Law and Disorder in the Postcolony* (pp. 1–56). Chicago, IL: University of Chicago Press.

Comaroff, J.L. and Comaroff, J. (2009) *Ethnicity Inc*. Chicago, IL: University of Chicago Press.

Comaroff, J. and Comaroff, J.L. (2012) *Theory from the South: Or, How Euro-America is Evolving Toward Africa*. Boulder, CO: Palgrave.

Couzens, T. (1985) *The New African: A Study of the Life and Work of H.I.E. Dhlomo*. Johannesburg: Ravan Press.

Cremers, J. and Gehring, R. (eds) (2013) *The Long and Winding Road to an Asbestos Free Workplace*. Brussels: CLR/International Books.

Crystal, D. (2003) *English as a Global Language*. Cambridge: Cambridge University Press.

CSS (2006) *Assessment of Environmental Contamination from Asbestos: Findings for the Former Asbestos Mining Regions of South Africa*. Grahamstown: Conservation Support Services.

Darnton, R. (1982) *The Literary Underground of the Old Regime*. Cambridge, MA: Harvard University Press.

Davis, C. and Johnson, D. (eds) (2015) *The Book in Africa: Critical Debates*. Basingstoke: Palgrave Macmillan.

Dempster, C. (1983a) South Africa under spotlight in anti-asbestos lobby. *The Star* (Johannesburg), 19 August, p. 3.

Dempster, C. (1983b) Warning by brokers on asbestos. *The Star* (Johannesburg), 25 August, p. 3.

Dempster, C. (1983c) Asbestos under siege. *Weekend Argus* (Johannesburg), 27 August, p. 6.

Dempster, C. (1984) Dismissed miners refuse to leave – but no action. *The Star* (Johannesburg), 27 July, p. 9.

Desmond, C. (1971) *The Discarded People: An Account of African Resettlement in South Africa*. Middlesex: Penguin.

Deutsch, J.-G., Probst, P. and Schmidt, H. (ed.) (2002) *African Modernities: Entangled Meanings in Current Debate*. Oxford: James Currey and Portsmouth: Heinemann.

Devitt, A. (2004) *Writing Genres*. Carbondale, IL: Southern Illinois University Press.

Drucker, P. (1969) *The Age of Discontinuity: Guidelines to Our Changing Society*. Oxford: Butterworth-Heinemann.

Duffy, A. (1997) Army base on old asbestos mine contaminated. *Mail & Guardian*, 12–18 September, p. 4.

Fabian, J. (1983) *Time and the Other: How Anthropology Constructs Us*. New York: Columbia University Press.

Fabian, J. (1990) *History from Below*. Amsterdam: John Benjamins.

Fabian, J. (1993) Keep listening: Ethnography and reading. In J. Boyarin (ed.) *The Ethnography of Reading* (pp. 80–97). Berkeley, CA: University of California Press.

Falender, J. (2002) The Cape plc Settlement: Analysis of the settlement terms and the future of asbestos litigation and compensation policy in South Africa. Unpublished paper, Brown University.

Felix, M.A., Leger, J.-P. and Ehrlich, R.I. (1994) Three minerals, three epidemics – asbestos mining and disease in South Africa. In M. Mehlman and J. Upton (eds) *The Identification and Control of Environmental and Occupational Disease* (pp. 265–286). Princeton, NJ: Princeton Scientific.

Ferguson, J. (2006) *Global Shadows: Africa in the Neoliberal World*. Durham, NC: Duke University Press.

Financial Mail Johannesburg (1989) Striking out on his own. *Financial Mail* (Johannesburg), 6 January.

Flynn, L. (1982) South Africa blacks out blue asbestos risk. *New Scientist*, 22 April, 237–239.

Foucault, M. (2009) *Security, Territory, Population: Lectures at the Collège de France, 1977–1978*. London: Picador.

Fraser, N. (1990) Rethinking the public sphere: A contribution to the critique of actually existing democracy. *Social Text* 25/26, 56–80.

Fraser, N. (2005) Reframing justice in a globalizing world. *New Left Review* 36, 73.

Friedman, S. (1983) Asbestos has been a 'major killer in South Africa. *Rand Daily Mail*, 19 August, p. 3.

Gibson, N. (2008) Black consciousness after Biko: The dialectics of liberation in South Africa, 1977–1987. In A. Mngxitama, A. Alexander and N. Gibson (eds) *Biko Lives! Contesting the Legacies of Steve Biko* (pp. 129–155). New York: Palgrave Macmillan.

Giteleman, L. (2014) *Paper Knowledge: Toward a Media History of Documents*. Durham, NC: Duke University Press.

Goldblatt, D. (2003) *Asbestos*. Stevenson Gallery, Cape Town, 1–25 October. See http://archive.stevenson.info/exhibitions/goldblatt/asbestos/asbestos.htm (accessed July 2017).

Goldblatt, D. (2005) *Intersections*. Munich: Prestel.

Gordon, C. (1991) Governmental rationality: An introduction. In G. Burchell, C. Gordon and P. Miller (eds) *The Foucault Effect: Studies in Governmentality* (pp. 1–51). Chicago, IL: University of Chicago Press.

Gramsci, A. (1971) *Selections from the Prison Notebooks* (ed. Q. Hoare and G.N. Smith). London: Lawrence & Wishart.

Gross, M. and McGoey, L. (eds) (2015) *Routledge International Handbook of Ignorance Studies*. London: Routledge.

Guha, R. and Martinez-Allier, J. (1997) *Varieties of Environmentalism: Essays North and South*. London: Earthscan.

Gumperz, J. (1992) Contextualization revisited. In P. Auer and A. Di Luzio (eds) *The Contextualization of Language* (pp. 39–53). Amsterdam: John Benjamins.

Guyton, G.P. (1999) A brief history of workers' compensation. *Iowa Orthopaedic Journal* 19, 106–110.

Hall, A.L. (1930) *Asbestos in the Union of South Africa*. Geological Survey Memoir No. 12. Pretoria: Government Printing Office.

Haworth-Booth, M. (2005) Interview with David Goldblatt. In D. Goldblatt *Intersections* (pp. 94–99). Munich: Prestel.

Heath, S.B. (1983) *Ways with Words: Language, Life and Work in Communities and Classrooms*. Cambridge: Cambridge University Press.

Horner, B. (1999) Re-thinking the 'sociality' of error: Teaching editing as negotiation. In B. Horner and M.-Z. Lu (eds) *Representing the 'Other': Basic Writers and the Teaching of Basic Writing* (pp. 139–165). Urbana, IL: NCTE.

Hull, M.S. (2012) Documents and bureaucracy. *Annual Review of Anthropology* 41, 251–267.

Hurst, E. (2009) Tsotsitaal, global culture and local style: Identity and recontextualisation in twenty-first century South African townships. *Social Dynamics* 35 (2), 244–257.

IBAS (International Ban Asbestos Secretariat) (2014) *Eternit and the Great Asbestos Trial*, 18 February. See http://www.ibasecretariat.org/eternit-great-asbestos-trial-toc.htm.

Jacob, M.-A. (2007) Form-made persons: Consent forms as consent's blind eye. *PoLAR: Political and Legal Anthropology Review* 30 (2), 249–268.

Jacobs, N.J. (2003) *Environment, Power, and Injustice: A South African History*. Cambridge: Cambridge University Press.

Johnson, R. (1979) 'Really useful knowledge': Radical education and working class culture, 1790–1848. In J. Clarke, C. Critcher and R. Johnson (eds) *Working Class Culture: Studies in History and Theory*. New York: St. Martin's.

Johnson, R. (1986–1987) What is cultural studies anyway? *Social Text* 16 (1), 38–80.

Kafka, B. (2009) Paperwork: The state of the discipline. *Book History* 12, 340–353.

Kafka, B. (2012) *The Demon of Writing: Powers and Failures of Paperwork*. Cambridge, MA: Harvard University Press.

Kapferer, J.-N. (1990) *Rumors: Uses, Interpretations, & Images*. New Brunswick, NJ: Transaction Publishers.

Kazan, L.A. (2000) Global asbestos justice: South African asbestos victims win right to sue Cape plc in UK. *Multinational Monitor* 21 (9). See http://www.multinationalmonitor.org/mm2000/092000/kazen-allen.html (accessed July 2017).

Koikanyang, L. (2010) Notorious lady cheats asbestos beneficiaries. *ITSE News*, 27 August–10 September.

Kotoloane, S. and Aitken, R. (2002) Presentation to the Northern Cape Provincial Asbestos Forum, 25 September.

Kress, G. and van Leeuwen, T. (1996) *Reading Images: The Grammar of Visual Design*. New York: Routledge.

Leburu, D. (2010) Malema promises to help Kuruman asbestosis victims. *Northern Cape News*, 1 June.

Ledwaba, L. (2018) Asbestos continues to kill as ex-miners fight for compensation. *Mail & Guardian*, 23 February. See https://mg.co.za/article/2018-02-23-00-asbestos-curse-continues-to-kill-as-ex-miners-fight-for-compensation.

Legassick, M. (2010) *The Politics of a South African Frontier: The Griqua, the Sotho-Tswana, and the Missionaries, 1780–1840*. Klosterberg: Basler Afrika Bibliographien.

Lillis, T. (2014) *The Sociolinguistics of Writing*. Edinburgh: Edinburgh University Press.

Lillis, T. and Curry, M.J. (2006) Professional academic writing by multilingual scholars: Interactions with literacy brokers in the production of English medium texts. *Written Communication* 23 (1), 3–35.

Lillis, T. and Curry, M.J. (2010) *Academic Writing in a Global Context: The Politics and Practices of Publishing in English*. London: Routledge.

Lillis, T. and McKinney, C. (2013) The sociolinguistics of writing in a global context. *Journal of Sociolinguistics* 17 (4), 415–439.

Makgabutiane, S. (1984) Dismissed strikers end sit-in at Penge. *The Star* (Johannesburg), 30 July, p. 7.

Makgabutiane, S. and Dempster, C. (1984) Mine strike still far from being resolved. *The Star* (Johannesburg), 14 July, p. 2.

Makhuda, K.D.P. (2002) An introduction to Flaaitaal (or Tsotsitaal). In R. Mesthrie (ed.) *Language in South Africa* (pp. 398–406). Cambridge: Cambridge University Press.

Malan, L. (1996) Literacy mediation and social identity in Newtown, Eastern Cape. In M. Prinsloo and M. Breirer (eds) *The Social Uses of Literacy* (pp. 105–122). Bertsham: SACHED Books.

Mamdani, M. (1996) *Citizen and Subject: Contemporary Africa and the Legacy of Late Colonialism*. Princeton, NJ: Princeton University Press.

Marais, H. (2011) *South Africa Pushed to the Limit: The Political Economy of Change*. London: Zed Books.

Masondo, S. (2017) Pomfret: The sins of the fathers. *City Press*, 15 January. See http://www.news24.com/SouthAfrica/News/pomfret-the-sins-of-the-fathers-20170115.

Maybin, J. (2017) Textual trajectories: Theoretical roots and institutional consequences. *Text & Talk* 37 (4), 415–435.

Mbingo, B. (2017) King sanctions opening of Bulembu mine. *Observer on Saturday*, 4 March. See https://www.pressreader.com/eswatini/observer-on-saturday/20170304/281483571170313

McCloud, S. (1993) *Understanding Comics: The Invisible Art*. New York: Harper Perennial.

McCulloch, J. (2002) *Asbestos Blues: Labour, Capital, Physicians & the State in South Africa*. Bloomington, IN: Indiana University Press.

McCulloch, J. (2003) Asbestos mining in Southern Africa, 1893–2002. *International Journal of Occupational and Environmental Health* 9 (3), 230–235.

McCulloch, J. (2005a) Asbestos, lies and the state: Occupational disease and South African science. *African Studies* 64 (2), 201–216.

McCulloch, J. (2005b) Beating the odds: The quest for justice by South African asbestos mining communities. *Review of African Political Economy* 32 (103), 63–77.

McCulloch, J. (2006) Saving the asbestos industry, 1960–2006. *Public Health Reports* 121, 609–614.

McCulloch, J. (2008) Surviving blue asbestos. *Transformation: Critical Perspectives on Southern Africa* 65, 68–93.

McCulloch, J. and Tweedale, G. (2008) *Defending the Indefensible: The Global Asbestos Industry and its Fight for Survival.* Oxford: Oxford University Press.

Mesthrie, R. and Hurst, E. (2013) Slang registers, code-switching and restructured urban varieties in South Africa: An overview of Tsotsitaals with special reference to the Cape Town variety. *Journal of Pidgin and Creole Languages* 28 (1), 103–130.

Mignolo, W.D. (2000) *Local Histories/Global Designs.* Princeton, NJ: Princeton University Press.

Mokae, G. (1989) Thirty years of silent murder ... the asbestos tragedy. *Frank Talk* 3, 62–66.

Morris, R. (2006) Gencor fades, but scars remain. *Business Report*, 5 February, p. 14.

Myers, J. (1980) Asbestos and asbestos-related disease in South Africa. SALDRU Working Paper No. 28. Cape Town: Southern Africa Labour and Development Research Unit.

Myers, J. (1981) The social context of occupational disease: Asbestos and South Africa. *International Journal of Health Services* 11 (2), 227–245.

Myers, J. and Steinberg, M. (1984) Health and safety: An emerging issue on the shop floor. *South African Review* 2.

Myers, J.E., Garisch, D., Myers, H.S., Cornell, J.E. and Rwexu, R.D. (1985) A respiratory epidemiological study of stevedores intermittently exposed to asbestos in a South African port. *American Journal of Industrial Medicine* 7 (4), 273–283.

National Asbestos Summit (1998) *Proceedings of the National Asbestos Summit, 24–26 November.* Johannesburg: National Parliamentary Portfolio Committee on Environment & Tourism.

Ndlovu, N., Naude, J. and Murray, J. (2013) Compensation for environmental asbestos-related diseases in South Africa: A neglected issue. *Global Health Action* 6, 82–88.

Nixon, R. (2014) *Slow Violence and the Environmentalism of the Poor.* Cambridge, MA: Harvard University Press.

Ntshangase, D.K. (2002) Language and language practices in Soweto. In R. Mesthrie (ed.) *Language in South Africa* (pp. 407–415). Cambridge: Cambridge University Press.

Petryna, A. (2002) *Life Exposed: Biological Citizenship After Chernobyl.* Princeton, NJ: Princeton University Press.

Pickles, J. (2004) *A History of Spaces: Cartographic Reason Mapping and the Geo-coded World.* New York: Routledge.

Piot, C. (1999) *Remotely Global: Village Modernity in West Africa.* Chicago, IL: University of Chicago Press.

Posel, D. (2000) A mania for measurement: Statistics and statecraft in the transition to apartheid. In S. Debow (ed.) *Science and Society in Southern Africa* (pp. 116–142). Manchester: Manchester University Press.

Pratt, M.L. (1987) Linguistic utopias. In C. MacCabe, N. Fabb, D. Attridge and A. Durant (eds) *The Linguistics of Writing: Arguments Between Language and Literature* (pp. 48–66). New York: Methuen.

Pratt, M.L. (2002) Modernity and periphery: Toward a global and relational analysis. In M. Elisabeth Mudimbe-Boyi (ed.) *Beyond Dichotomies: Histories, Identities, Cultures, and the Challenge of Globalization* (pp. 21–48). Albany, NY: State University of New York Press.

Proctor, R. (1995) *Cancer Wars: How Politics Shapes What We Know and Don't Know about Cancer.* New York: Basic Books.

Proctor, R. and Schiebinger, L. (eds) (1995) *Agnotology: The Making and Unmaking of Ignorance.* Palo Alto, CA: Stanford University Press.

Rand Daily Mail (1983) Safety law: Is it safe? *Rand Daily Mail*, 19 August, p. 6.

Rice, J. (2011) The global reorganization and revitalization of the asbestos industry, 1970–2007. *International Journal of Health Services* 41 (2), 239–254.

Roberts, A. (2007) *The Wonga Coup: Guns, Thugs, and a Ruthless Determination to Create Mayhem in an Oil-rich Corner of Africa.* New York: Public Affairs Books.

Roberts, J. (2009) *The Hidden Epidemic Amongst Former Miners: Silicosis, Tuberculosis, and the Occupational Diseases in Mines and Works Act in the Eastern Cape, South Africa.* Durban: Health Systems Trust.

Robins, S. (1996) Cultural brokers and bricoleurs of modern and traditional literacies: Land struggles in Namaqualand's coloured reserves. In M. Prinsloo and M. Breirer (eds) *The Social Uses of Literacy* (pp. 123–140). Bertsham: SACHED Books.

SALB (1983) Occupational health service groups. *South African Labour Bulletin* 8 (7), 20–25.

Schapera, I. (1970) *Tribal Innovators: Tswana Chiefs and Social Change 1795–1940.* London: Bloomsbury Academic.

Schepers, G.W.H. (1965) Discussion. *Biological Effects of Asbestos. Annals of the New York Academy of Sciences* 132, 595–596.

Schwartze, S. (2007) Silences and the possibilities of asbestos activism: Stories from Libby. In R.D. Sandler and P.C. Pezzullo (eds) *Environmental Justice and Environmentalism: The Social Justice Challenge to the Environmental Movement* (pp. 165–187). Cambridge. MA: MIT Press.

Shillington, K. (1985) *The Colonisation of the Southern Tswana 1870–1900.* Braamfontein: Ravan Press.

Shillington, K. (2011) *Luka Jantjie: Resistance Hero of the South African Frontier.* London: Aldridge Press.

Silverstein, M. and Urban, G. (1996) The natural history of discourse. In M. Silverstein and G. Urban (eds) *Natural Histories of Discourse* (pp. 1–20). Chicago, IL: University of Chicago Press.

Simson, F.W. (1928) Pulmonary asbestosis in South Africa. *British Medical Journal* 1 (3516), 885–887.

Snyman, P.H.R. (1988) Safety and health in the Northern Cape blue asbestos belt. *Historia* 33, 31–52.

Social Dynamics (1978) *Social Dynamics* 4 (2).

South African Labour Bulletin (1979) *South African Labour Bulletin* 4 (9 &10).

Spoor (n.d.) Memorandum to Counsel. Unpublished paper.

Spoor, R. (2001a) The Cape asbestos claims. Unpublished paper, February.

Spoor, R. (2001b) Workman's compensation and the prevalence of occupational injuries and disease in South Africa. Unpublished paper, July.

Spoor, R. (2003a) The social consequences of mining in South Africa in the past and in the future. Unpublished paper, June.

Spoor, R. (2003b) Civil law consequences of an employer's failure to create a safe and healthy work environment. Unpublished paper, July.

Statistics South Africa (2012a) *Census 2011: Statistical Release.* Pretoria: Statistics South Africa.

Statistics South Africa (2012b) *Census 2011: Provinces at a Glance.* Pretoria: Statistics South Africa.

Stewart, P. and Jennings, R. (2007) *'Great Expectations': Expenditure Patterns and Assessment of Asbestos Relief Trust Compensation Awards.* Johannesburg: Asbestos Relief Trust.

Sunday Times Johannesburg (1989) Gefco the Star of My Portfolio. *Sunday Times* (Johannesburg), 2 July, p. 2.

teWaterNaude, J.M. (2014) The story of the asbestos relief trust – Part 1. *Occupational Health Southern Africa* 20 (1), 4–5.

Thompson, L. (2001) *A History of South Africa.* New Haven, CT: Yale University Press.

Toffler, A. (1970) *Future Shock.* New York: Random House.

Tracks4Africa (n.d.) Msauli, abandoned town & asbestos mine. *Tracks4Africa.* https://tracks4africa.co.za/listings/photo_gallery/w169188/ (accessed July 2017).

Trimbur, J. (2001) Popular literacy: Caught between art and crime. In J. Trimbur (ed.) *Popular Literacy: Studies in Cultural Practices and Poetics* (pp. 1–16). Pittsburgh, PA: University of Pittsburgh Press.

Trimbur, J. (2002) Language policy and normalization in South Africa: Some other lessons. *JAC: Journal of Composition Theory* 22 (3), 646–657.

Trimbur, J. (2009) English in a splintered metropolis: South Africa after apartheid. *JAC: A Quarterly Journal for the Interdisciplinary Study of Rhetoric, Writing, Multiple Literacies, and Politics* 29 (1–2), 107–137.

Trimbur, J. (2011) *Solidarity or Service: Composition and the Problem of Expertise.* Portsmouth, NH: Heinemann, 2011.

Tsing, A.L. (2005) *Friction: An Ethnography of Global Connection.* Princeton, NJ: Princeton University Press.

Tweedale, G. (2000) *Magic Mineral to Killer Dust: Turner & Newall and the Asbestos Hazard.* Oxford: Oxford University Press.

Urban, G. (1996) Entextualization, replication, and power. In M. Silverstein and G. Urban (eds) *Natural Histories of Discourse* (pp. 21–44). Chicago, IL: University of Chicago Press.

van der Vlies, A. (ed.) (2012) *Print, Text and Book Culture in South Africa.* Johannesburg: Wits University Press.

van Horssen, J. (2016) *A Town Called Asbestos: Environmental Contamination, Health, and Resilience in a Resource Community.* Vancouver: University of British Columbia.

Visage, N. (2007) Scores forced to flee from asbestos threat. *Diamond Fields Observer*, 29 March, p. 4.

Wagner, J.C. (1986) Mesothelioma and mineral fibres. *Cancer* 57 (10), 1905–1911.

Wagner, J.C., Sleggs, C.A. and Marchand, P. (1960) Diffuse pleural mesothelioma and asbestos exposure in the North West Cape Province. *British Journal of Industrial Medicine* 17 (4), 260–271.

Waldman, L. (2007) When social movements bypass the poor: Asbestos pollution, international litigation and Griqua cultural identity. *Journal of Southern African Studies* 33 (3), 577–600.

Waldman, L. (2011) *The Politics of Asbestos: Understandings of Risk, Disease and Protest.* London: Earthscan and New York: Routledge.

Warner, M. (2005) *Publics and Counter Publics.* Cambridge: Zone Books.

Weavind, T. (2014) Playing in the shadow of asbestos mine dumps. *Mail & Guardian*, 5 September. See https://mg.co.za/article/2014-09-04-playing-in-the-shadow-of-asbestos-mine-dumps

Willan, B. (1984) *Sol Plaatje: South African Nationalist, 1876–1932.* London: Heinemann.

Wilson, F. (1978) Overview. *Social Dynamics* 4 (2), 155.

Wits (2012) *Roots of BC Trade Unionism.* Johannesburg: Wits Historical Papers, University of Witwatersrand. See http://www.historicalpapers.wits.ac.za/inventories/inv_pdfo/AK2117/AK2117-J2-25-Z12-002-jpeg.pdf (accessed July 2017).

Wits (n.d.) *David Goldblatt (Born 1930).* Johannesburg: Adler Medical Museum, University of the Witwatersrand. See https://www.wits.ac.za/health/adlermuseum/exhibitions/david-goldblatt-born-1930/ (accessed July 2017).

Yates, J. (1993) *Control through Communication: The Rise of System in American Management.* Baltimore, MD: Johns Hopkins University Press.

Index

For Product Safety Concerns and Information please contact our EU Authorised Representative:

Easy Access System Europe

Mustamäe tee 50

10621 Tallinn

Estonia

gpsr.requests@easproject.com

www.ingramcontent.com/pod-product-compliance
Ingram Content Group UK Ltd.
Pitfield, Milton Keynes, MK11 3LW, UK
UKHW021839230925
3041IPUK00002B/2